To my mother,
who has a new story for me every single day.

AF543407

FROM SUNRISE
TO
SALVATION

FROM SUNRISE TO SALVATION

What Ancient India Knew about Love, Sex, Society, and the Soul

AVANEESH

HAY HOUSE

HAY HOUSE INDIA
New Delhi • London • Sydney
Carlsbad, California • New York City

Copyright © Avaneesh 2026

Hay House Publishers (India) Pvt Ltd
Muskaan Complex, Plot No. 3, B-2, Vasant Kunj, New Delhi – 110070, India

Hay House LLC, P.O. Box 5100, Carlsbad, CA 92018-5100, USA
Hay House UK Ltd, 1st Floor, Crawford Corner, 91-93 Baker Street, London W1U 6QQ, UK
Hay House Australia Publishing Pty Ltd, 18/36 Ralph St., Alexandria NSW 2015, Australia

Email: contact@hayhouse.co.in
Website: www.hayhouse.co.in

The views and opinions expressed in this book are the author's own and the facts are as reported by him. They have been verified to the extent possible, and the publishers are not in any way liable for the same.

All rights reserved. No part of this publication may be reproduced, by any mechanical, photographic, or electronic process, or in the form of a phonographic recording, nor may it be stored in a retrieval system, transmitted, or otherwise be copied for public or private use – other than for 'fair use' as brief quotations embodied in articles and reviews – without prior written permission of the publisher.

The author of this book does not dispense medical advice or prescribe the use of any technique as a form of treatment for physical, emotional, or medical problems without the advice of a physician, either directly or indirectly. The intent of the author is only to offer information of a general nature to help you in your quest for emotional, physical, and spiritual well-being. In the event you use any of the information in this book for yourself, the author and the publisher assume no responsibility for your actions.

First published by Hay House India, 2026
10 9 8 7 6 5 4 3 2 1

ISBN 978-93-6611-381-4 (Paperback)
ISBN 978-93-6611-831-4 (Ebook)

Cover illustration by Rahul Jayasree

Printed at Replika Press Pvt. Ltd.

MIX
Paper | Supporting responsible forestry
FSC™ C016779
FSC www.fsc.org

Hay House is committed to a sustainable future for our business, our readers and our planet. This book is made from Forest Stewardship Council® certified paper.

CONTENTS

'There was neither death nor immortality then,
No discriminating sign of night nor of day,
That One breathed, windless, by its own impulse,
There was that One, and there was no other.

Darkness there was at first, by darkness hidden,
All this was unillumined cosmic water,
That which, becoming, by the void was covered,
That One, by force of knowledge, came into being.

Who really knows? Who will here proclaim it?
Whence it all came? How was this creation?
Gods came afterwards, with the creation of this universe.
Who then knows whence it has arisen?

Whether God's will created it, or whether He was mute,
Perhaps it formed itself, perhaps it did not,
He who perceives it all from the highest skies,
He knows it, or even he does not.'

—Rigveda

INTRODUCTION

Since this book offers a unique perspective on the many facets of ancient Indian life, I wanted to begin not with an academic exposition, but with something different—something that could immediately immerse the reader in the spirit of the ideas explored here. I have therefore chosen to open with a story, an allegory that sets the stage for the book, introducing the themes of self, observation, and the timeless wisdom that underlies daily life in ancient India.

Two birds sit on the same tree. They are inseparable companions.

One bird perches on the lower branch. Restless. Busy.

It hops from twig to twig, pecking at the fruits of the tree—some sweet, some bitter. It eats, reacts, suffers, enjoys, and keeps searching. When the fruit is sweet, it is happy. When it is bitter, the bird is miserable. Yet it cannot stop eating.

The other bird sits on the upper branch. Silent. Still. Radiant. It does not eat. It does not react. It simply watches.

Now and then, after tasting a particularly bitter fruit, the lower bird looks up. It notices the other bird, calm, untouched by sweetness or sorrow. For a moment, it feels drawn to it. But then another fruit catches its eye, and it goes back to eating.

Again and again this happens: sweetness, bitterness, joy, grief, excitement, disappointment. And every time the suffering becomes too sharp, it glances upward at that serene companion.

Gradually, very gradually, it begins to move higher on the tree. Branch by branch.

As it comes closer, something strange happens. The radiant bird on the upper branch seems less like another and more like itself. Until finally, the lower bird reaches the top and realises there were never two birds at all.

The bird that was eating the fruits—*jivatman* (the individual self)—and the bird that was only witnessing *paramatman* (the universal self)—were always the same. One lost in experience and the other one free from it.

This allegory from the Mundaka Upanishad captures the essence of human life as ancient Indians understood it. You are not only the one tasting every sweet and bitter fruit, experiencing joy and sorrow. You are also the one who can rise above it all—silent, observant, and unattached—witnessing life without being bound by it.

Remember, true liberation begins the moment you recognise this inner freedom and embrace your role as both participant and witness. The path is always before you, and now it is your turn to take the first step.

Chapter 1

WAKING AND ENERGY

'Arise! Awake! Approach the great and learn.'
—Katha Upanishad

Brahma Muhurtam: Time for Waking and Awakening

The ancient Indians were pioneers of holistic living, and this approach began from the very moment they rose each day. In fact, they did not wake up in the morning as we commonly understand it; they woke up before the morning. Why rise so early? What was the significance of this pre-dawn hour? To understand this, we need to look at the sacred time window they considered most conducive to physical, mental, and spiritual well-being.

Since Vedic times, the ancient Indians have regarded the early pre-dawn hours as especially sacred, rising during an auspicious period known as *Brahma Muhurtam*. This 48-minute window begins 1 hour and 36 minutes before sunrise and concludes 48 minutes before sunrise. For instance, if sunrise occurs at 6:00 a.m., Brahma Muhurtam would extend from 4:24 a.m. to 5:12 a.m.

In the traditional Vedic division of time, the night is segmented into 15 Muhurtams, each lasting 48 minutes. Brahma Muhurtam is the fourteenth and the penultimate *muhurtam* of the night. Considered the most auspicious time of the entire day for yogic, spiritual, and intellectual pursuits, it literally translates to 'the time of Brahma,' the deity of creation. The enlightened seers of ancient India described this period as ideal for awakening, believing that during these quiet moments before dawn, the human mind and body exist in a pristine state of subtle balance.

And today, modern science has validated this ancient Indian wisdom. Research shows that the pineal gland secretes the hormone melatonin at optimum levels during this time, and melatonin is believed to have a mood-stabilising effect. The anti-stress hormone cortisol, too, is secreted at optimal levels during these early hours. And according to the *International Journal of Yoga and Allied Sciences*, nascent oxygen is said to be available in the atmosphere during Brahma Muhurtam, and upon breathing, it is known to positively impact the body by increasing energy levels and boosting immunity. Additionally, the 1,500-year-old Ayurvedic text *Ashtanga Hridayam*, written by the brilliant Vagbhatta, states that waking up during Brahma Muhurtam is the key to a long and healthy life.

It is precisely for these reasons that ancient Indians chose this sacred window to awaken and engage in spiritual, meditative, and introspective practices. Is it not awe-inspiring to realise that our ancestors possessed such a nuanced understanding of the human body and mind thousands of years ago?

It naturally follows, then, that this period was reserved for activities aligned with such heightened awareness. Thus, the following activities are believed to yield maximal benefits when undertaken during Brahma Muhurtam: yogic meditation, studying and other forms of learning, creative pursuits such as writing and painting, as well as reflection and introspection. This is because it is a time when the subtler aspect of the self is at its highest potential, and it is this subtle dimension that we are meant to cultivate, refine, and nurture. However, activities involving intense physical exertion are discouraged during this muhurtam.

Seen in this light, the sanctity of this hour extends beyond mere practice and into the very spirit with which the day is begun. It may therefore be understood as a sacred hour imbued with immense creative potential—a time to shape oneself into one's true, magnificent form. To begin the day with the awareness that such boundless possibilities reside within is nothing short of sublime. Perhaps that is why ancient Indians, upon waking during Brahma Muhurtam, would look at their open palms and chant the mantra:

'Karaagre vasate Lakshmi
Kara madhye Saraswati
Kara moole sthitho Gauri
Prabhaate kara darshana.'

This mantra translates to: 'At the tip of my hand resides Lakshmi, the goddess of abundance; in the middle of my hand resides Saraswati, the goddess of wisdom; at the base of my hand resides Gauri, the goddess of inner strength. Thus, at dawn, I behold my hands.'

In uttering these words upon waking, every Indian gently reminded oneself that within one's own hands lies unfathomable power to create, to learn, to persevere, and ultimately, to achieve anything through one's own effort. This daily affirmation was not a mere poetic utterance, but a reflection of an integrated worldview. Indeed, the very fact that the ancient Indian seers chose to invoke the divine feminine at the first moment of waking reveals a profound insight: for them, waking was not merely a biological act, but an awakening. To channel the creative power of Brahma, those ingenious scholars invoked the goddesses, embodying the harmonious symbiosis of *prakriti* and *purusha*—the feminine and the masculine principles of existence. In doing so, they infused a seemingly simple daily ritual with high philosophy, deep spirituality, and a timeless vision of gender complementarity.

Thus, every Brahma Muhurtam becomes more than just a time of day; it is an auspicious invitation to not only wake but to awaken.

Surya Namaskaram: Eternal Energy from the Heavens

The ancient Indians were panentheistic. Meaning, they perceived divinity in everything. This reverence was especially evident in their relationship with the forces of nature—the primordial manifestations of existence. After waking and before setting foot upon the floor, they would touch the ground with their right hand, bring that hand to their forehead in reverence, and silently chant a mantra—an apology to Mother Earth for stepping upon her. Only then would they allow their feet to touch the ground.

Observe the beautiful contrast in this ritual. They opened their eyes and affirmed that within their own hands resided the power of the universe. And in the very next moment, they bowed to the earth in apology. The reason for this was that, as the first conscious act of the day, it served as a reminder that humility should always accompany power.

Having paid obeisance to Mother Earth with their gaze lowered, they would then lift their eyes upward to the sun and perform *Surya Namaskaram*. Literally translated as 'sun salutation,' it is an act of bowing to the sun in gratitude for sustaining life on earth.

It is worth noting that Surya Namaskaram is a meticulously designed sequence of twelve powerful yoga postures, or asanas, with profound effects on the human body and mind. The number twelve is no accident. The solar cycle spans approximately twelve and a quarter years. The wise seers of ancient India structured these twelve asanas to cultivate within the practitioner a subtle alignment with the sun's rhythms in order to synchronise the human system with the larger cosmic cycle. Here, you may ask: Why is this synchronisation so significant? Let's take a closer look at it.

Surya (sun) finds mention in the Rigveda, which is among the oldest known spiritual and philosophical texts, compiled around 3,500 years ago. It is also referenced in the Upanishads, which associate surya with sight and knowledge, and in the Mahabharata, which honours it as the 'eye of the universe.' And as the *karmasakshi*—the witness of all actions—it is also revered as a symbol of awakening our inner vision through reflection and meditation.

In addition to this, the ancient Indians identified surya as the source of all life and the eternal wellspring of energy. They regarded it as the creator of the material universe—prakriti—thereby emphasising the importance of harmonising our physical existence with the solar force.

Additionally, they understood that the body is both a stepping-stone to extraordinary possibilities and, paradoxically, a hurdle when left unrefined. By synchronising the body with the solar cycle, it becomes balanced, receptive, and no longer an obstacle. Surya Namaskaram thus emerges as a powerful technique to open oneself to the light and vitality of the sun, to internalise its essence, and to prepare the body as fertile ground for both material achievement and spiritual awakening. This inner equilibrium, once established, expands into a cosmic harmony as the core of the individual aligns with the greater rhythm of the universe, bridging the internal and external dimensions of existence.

This careful alignment of body and sun not only nurtures vitality but also sets the stage for practical benefits in physical health. When performed mindfully—with conscious breathing and appropriate chanting—Surya Namaskaram transforms into a complete cardiovascular exercise regime. It is even said that this process stretches every muscle in the human body, including the delicate muscles of the middle ear.

Beyond its physical benefits, Surya Namaskaram also prepares the mind and spirit for the deeper demands of life in the Kali Yuga. In this age, marked by unique challenges and mental unrest, the ancient gurus emphasised that divinity remains accessible, provided yoga is approached not merely as contemplation, but as disciplined *kriya*, that is, purposeful physical action grounded in asana. For over 5,000 years, our ancestors have recognised this and, in turn, wove Surya Namaskaram into daily life as a vital practice. This is significant because, by fully engaging the body, we lay the foundation for harmonising the subtle mind and, ultimately, begin to perceive the divine within.

The chapter 'Yuddha Kandam' of the Ramayana recounts how the sage Agastya imparted the sacred hymn Adityahridayam—the heart of the sun—to Rama, granting him the inner strength to overcome his formidable enemy. If the noble Rama performed sun worship in the comparatively purer Treta Yuga, imagine the necessity for us, living in the spiritually and morally turbulent Kali Yuga, to embrace this unparalleled practice.

It thus becomes evident that the ancient Indians consciously combined two powerful disciplines at the very dawn of their day—one to awaken the mind, and the other to invigorate the body. Yet the wisdom of the ancients extended beyond these practices alone. They understood that once awake, our conscious engagements are largely directed towards the external world. To move through life meaningfully, we must first establish balance between the internal and external universes. When the mind, the body, and the world around us are in synchrony, the foundation is set. What follows, then, is our attitude, and it is here that the true transformation begins. Beginning the day during Brahma Muhurtam, performing Surya Namaskaram with reverence, and cultivating gratitude towards the universe, coupled with confidence in our own creative potential, nurtures a positivity and serenity that can sustain us throughout the day. When humility, harmony, and self-belief converge, the ordinary morning transforms into a sacred commencement.

Contrast this with our present reality. We live in an age defined by lifestyle disorders like diabetes and obesity, where the relentless pace of modern life keeps the mind under constant stress and pressure. Is it not, then, time to restore these invaluable ancient practices of rising during Brahma Muhurtam and performing Surya Namaskaram to our daily routine, especially when our lives are saturated with unhealthy habits and unending strain? Yes, it is time to reclaim what we have neglected and realign ourselves with a way of living that restores balance, vitality, and inner clarity.

Takeaways from the Ancient Past

- Waking during the auspicious Brahma Muhurtam is the most conducive way to engage in spiritual and introspective practices. It is the hour when the mind is at its purest and ready to discover the divine within.
- Performing Surya Namaskaram at sunrise is among the most complete forms of cardiovascular exercise for the body. When practised correctly, this ancient discipline prepares the body to actualise the extraordinary possibilities that lie dormant within.
- Beginning the day with humility and gratitude towards nature and its resources is the most sublime way to harmonise spirituality with sustainability. This rare synthesis was conceived, refined, and lived by the luminous minds of ancient India for centuries. All that remains for us is to imbibe it, introspect upon it, and integrate it into our daily lives in our own sincere and conscious way.

Chapter 2

CLEANSING AND RENEWAL

'The body is indeed the primary instrument for the practice of dharma.'
—Charaka Samhita

Bathing: A Process beyond Cleansing

India is a land abundantly blessed by nature with thousands of pristine water bodies that have flowed across its length and breadth for millennia. To the ancient Indians—who revered the forces of nature—water was not merely a resource; it was the holiest of the holy. Their relationship with water thus transcended the utilitarian and entered the realm of the sacred. This reverence was not confined to belief alone but found expression in their daily rituals.

Bathing, in this context, was regarded as a *sadhana*—a spiritual discipline undertaken with intention and awareness. It was not simply an act of washing the body but a conscious process of self-cleansing that refined both the outer and inner being. The morning bath, in particular, was considered auspicious, as it marked a moment of renewal in which gratitude towards nature and responsibility towards oneself converged. The body was seen as a temple that houses the soul, and caring for it was both a personal duty and a sacred offering. This understanding naturally shaped the manner in which the ritual itself was performed.

Thus, after acknowledging the earth and lifting their gaze to the sky, they would turn at dawn to forge a conscious connection with the element of water, thereby marking the beginning of the morning bathing ritual in ancient India. For this purpose, they would proceed to the nearest river or to the pond in their village or city, which was a water reservoir constructed by rulers since prehistoric times. These public ponds collected pure rainwater, offering communities access to water in its most unadulterated form.

Since bathing was not merely an act of physical cleansing but a profound and holistic process of purification, it was performed in a ritualistic manner. The ritual began with the individual entering the water up to the waist, cupping both hands to gather the water, lifting it reverentially towards nature, and chanting:

> *'Gange cha Yamune chaiva Godhavari*
> *Saraswati Narmade Sindhu Kaveri*
> *Jalesmin sannidhim kuru.'*
> (O Ganga, Yamuna, Godhavari, Saraswati, Narmada, Sindhu, Kaveri, please come and reside in this water.)

Through this invocation, the devotee called upon the sacred rivers to sanctify the water before him. In doing so, the ancients affirmed that every body of water is holy, worthy of reverence. They recognised that through the element of water, all rivers and reservoirs are interconnected, forming one continuous cosmic essence. By attributing divinity to water, they simultaneously assumed responsibility for preserving its purity, protecting it as one would protect the divine itself. Bathing, therefore, became both a responsibility towards nature and a duty towards oneself, preserving the external world while nourishing the inner being.

It is noteworthy that, unlike in many other parts of the world, bathing was a daily discipline in ancient India. So integral was this practice that even early Western observers are said to have marvelled at the sight of people bathing each day in rivers such as the Kaveri in Tamil Nadu, gradually realising that this was not an occasional custom but a way of life. In fact, in ancient India, the preparations for bathing were often more elaborate than the act of bathing itself. This included oil massage and the use of specific ingredients, as shown below.

1. **Abhyanga (Oil Massage)**

   Since time immemorial, Indians have been renowned for preparing some of the finest hair oils. Their luxuriant black hair has long stood as living testimony to this mastery, reflecting a tradition rooted in both knowledge and daily practice. Depending on the geographical region, they chose coconut, sesame, or mustard oil as the base. Into these freshly pressed oils, they infused a variety of herbs known to promote hair growth, strengthen the roots, preserve natural colour, cleanse the scalp, maintain lustre, and enhance blood circulation.

   These potent formulations were meticulously documented in Ayurvedic texts compiled thousands of years ago and preserved even earlier through rich oral traditions. The oils were customised according to individual hair types and bodily constitutions. Warmed and applied with care, they were massaged into the scalp until the pores opened to absorb their nourishment. Bathing would typically follow 45 minutes to an hour later, allowing the oil to work its subtle magic.

   This oil massage was not confined to the head alone. The body, too, was anointed with specially prepared oils designed to enhance radiance, maintain suppleness, keep the skin firm and infection-free, and impart a gentle, natural fragrance. In Ayurveda, this practice is known as *abhyanga*. Traditionally performed by two individuals standing on either side—though it can also be self-administered—abhyanga improves circulation, lubricates joints, reduces stress, promotes restful sleep, detoxifies the body, and offers deep rejuvenation.

2. Shampoos and Scrubs

Soaps were never integral to the traditional Indian cleansing routine. Even thousands of years ago, these astute practitioners understood that harsh, soapy substances could harm the skin over time. Instead, they developed *choornam* (herbal powders) and *lepam* (herbal pastes) for cleansing and exfoliation.

Commonly used powders included *vetiver* (Chrysopogon), *manjishta* (*Rubia cordifolia*), *yashtimadhu* (liquorice), Bengal gram flour, and green gram flour. Vetiver, remarkably, was even used as a natural loofah. Among the widely used pastes were *haridra* (turmeric), *chandanam* (sandalwood), and *rakta chandanam* (red sandalwood). Turmeric, besides imparting a luminous glow, serves as a powerful antimicrobial agent, keeping the skin healthy and disease-free. Tamarind paste was occasionally applied as well, valued for its natural de tanning and exfoliating properties.

The ancient Indians also formulated exceptional organic shampoos that left their hair clean, fragrant, and glossy. The leaves and flowers of hibiscus, along with the leaves of *bala* (Sida cordifolia), were among the most popular ingredients. When ground, these herbs produced a thick, viscous preparation that, once massaged into the scalp, deeply cleansed it, strengthened the hair roots, reduced inflammation, and imparted a natural sheen.

Even today, one may glimpse the spirit of this tradition by bathing in cool water early in the morning and using at least one natural preparation made by one's own hands, something as simple as crushing hibiscus leaves into a gentle herbal shampoo. And even if time permits only a few minutes, approaching the bath as a form of meditation—honouring the body through nature's crystalline waters—reveals the difference between an ordinary wash and a true *snanam* (proper bathing).

Thus, we can see that in ancient India, bathing was not merely a matter of hygiene but a carefully structured ritual that artfully fused health, discipline, reverence, and inner refinement. In the next section, we will explore how this ritual functioned as a spiritual and therapeutic discipline, thoughtfully adapted to different life stages and roles, and designed to integrate physical cleansing, internal purification, and a deeper alignment with nature.

Ritual and Renewal: The Philosophy of Cleansing

As a rule, ancient Indians generally bathed twice daily, once in the early morning and again around sunset, before their twilight prayers and reflections. However, Ayurveda prescribed variations in bathing frequency depending on one's profession, constitution, and health. The Vedas suggest that a *brahmacharini* (female householder) bathe once daily, while a male householder bathes twice, before sunrise and again in the afternoon after work. *Sanyasis*, or renunciates, were advised to bathe three times a day—before sunrise, at noon, and before sunset. This regimen was intended to regulate bodily heat, calm the senses, and steady both physical and mental impulses.

There were also distinct bathing procedures prescribed for pregnant women and for the post-partum period. After childbirth, mothers were given baths in warm, herb-infused medicated water, often accompanied by a gentle steam bath. This therapeutic process was designed to restore vitality, strengthen the uterine and vaginal muscles, and rejuvenate the body after the intense experience of childbirth.

As for those who embraced a yogic lifestyle, purification extended beyond the external body. Alongside physical cleansing was the concept of internal purification, known as *shuddhi*. This involved the disciplined use of clean water for practices such as nasal cleansing (*neti*), upper digestive tract cleansing (*dhauti*), and colon cleansing (*basti*). This highlights how, in ancient India, water was not merely a cleansing agent for the skin but a medium for profound internal renewal.

Additionally, families belonging to the upper strata of society often had private ponds adjacent to their homes, replenished continuously by underground springs and rainwater. For the wider public, rulers constructed expansive bathing ponds known as *snana ghattams*, accessible to all free of cost. Beyond these, the land itself was interwoven with rivers, lakes, and streams, offering abundant opportunities for daily ablutions. Other than this, sophisticated bathing facilities were present in urban centres as early as 2,500 BCE, most notably the Great Bath of the Indus Valley Civilisation at Mohenjo-daro, which is an enduring testament to the importance accorded to ritual purity and hygiene.

Viewed in this light, the bathing traditions of ancient India formed an integrated system of daily regulation and care. They reflected an intimate understanding of the body's rhythms, the demands of different paths in life, and the restorative power of water. What emerges is a civilisation in which cleanliness, vitality, composure, and spiritual refinement were sustained through conscious and consistent practice, where bathing was not merely an act of hygiene but a disciplined dialogue between the individual, nature, and the sacred.

Takeaways from the Ancient Past

- Every bath should begin with an expression of gratitude and reverence towards water, fostering an intimate bond with nature. This relationship nurtures responsibility and sustainability, encouraging us to value and protect water, which is one of our most precious resources.
- Viewing bathing as both external and internal purification transforms it into a daily ritual of renewal. It refreshes not only the body but also the mind, becoming a natural practice of relaxation and de-stressing.
- Using bathing products sourced directly from nature is a powerful way to preserve the health and vitality of our skin and hair. Preparing even a simple product oneself instils creativity and self-reliance, energising daily life with a quiet confidence.

Chapter 3

CLOTHING AND CONSCIOUSNESS

'When the body is in fine clothes, the reflection is also in fine clothes. If the body is destroyed, the reflection is gone.'
—Chandogya Upanishad

Vastram: Sartorial Revolution in Ancient India

In the earlier chapter, we explored how the morning bath formed an integral ritual in ancient India, preparing the body and mind for the day ahead. This was followed by adorning oneself in clean, freshly washed, and sun-dried garments. In harmony with the climatic realities of the subcontinent, ancient Indians emphasised the principle of air in their clothing. They chose breathable fabrics that allowed generous circulation—an essential adaptation to the tropical climate. Thus, after invoking the sky, the earth, and the waters, they consciously integrated air into their daily living through what they wore.

To truly understand the history of clothing in India, we must journey back nearly 7,000 years to the Indus Valley Civilisation, where cotton was already being spun, woven, and dyed with remarkable skill. Archaeological excavations have revealed bone needles and wooden spindles at several Indus sites, testifying to a thriving textile culture. Contrary to popular assumption, the cotton industry in ancient India was extraordinarily advanced. Many of the sophisticated techniques developed then continue to survive even today.

The ancient Greek historian Herodotus described Indian cotton as 'a wool exceeding in beauty and goodness to that of sheep.' Known in Sanskrit as *karpasa*, Indian cotton was so prized that it was exported widely to major kingdoms of both the East and the West. Indeed, ancient Indians were among the earliest—and perhaps the very first—cotton weavers in human history.

Ancient India also produced some of the finest linen the world had ever known. The Greek voyager Nearchus and the historian Arrian recorded that Indian linen was whiter and softer than any they had encountered. Referred to in Sanskrit as *kshauma*, linen is mentioned frequently in the Vedas, Puranas, and Upanishads. It was regarded as pure, sacred, and a symbol of refinement and royalty.

Such was the esteem in which this fabric was held that it found a place not only in daily life but also in sacred literature and ritual. The *Acaranga* recounts how Sakra presented Mahavira with a piece of linen so delicate that it could be lifted by a gentle breeze. Ayurveda prescribes that newborns be wrapped in linen cloth and that post-partum bedding be made of linen, emphasising its purity and comfort. The *Grihya Sutra Kandika* records a regulation around 500 BCE instructing students to wear linen or hemp (*sana*) garments upon initiation into student life. Even in the Ramayana, Ravana's mortal remains are described as being clothed in linen before cremation. Thus, from cradle to grave, linen symbolised sanctity and serenity.

There is also archaeological evidence of silk being used as early as the Harappan period. Analysis of silk fibres from these sites suggests that the threads were produced through reeling—a technique long believed to have been exclusive to China until the first century

CE. Known in Sanskrit as *kausheya*, silk was rare, luxurious, and reserved for the privileged.

Dyeing in ancient India was equally sophisticated. Artisans identified five primary colours known as *shuddha varnas*, along with innumerable composite shades called *misra varnas*, categorised with astonishing precision. The ancient treatise *Vishnu Dharmottara* distinguishes five distinct shades of white: jasmine, ivory, the August moon, August clouds after rain, and the conch shell. This reveals a refined sensitivity to even the subtlest tonal variations.

Additionally, sources of dyes were meticulously derived from nature—plants, minerals, and even certain animal products. Among them were *nila* (indigo), *manjishta* (madder), *lodhra*, *haridra* (turmeric), *maharanjana* (safflower), *kumkuma* (saffron), *kerme* (kermes), *recona* (a bright yellow pigment), *gairica* (red ochre), and *khanjana* (carbon black), among many others.

Thus, it becomes evident that clothing in ancient India was not merely a functional necessity but an artistic, scientific, and spiritual expression—an elegant assimilation of nature's elements into the very fabric of daily life.

Threads of Civilisation: The Philosophy of Clothing in Ancient India

In ancient India, the garments one wore reflected a deeper philosophy of living in harmony with nature and circumstance. Put simply, dress was never incidental; it was deliberate. And unlike today, when fashion trends are often followed without reflection, ancient Indians dressed in accordance with their lifestyle and profession, ensuring comfort without sacrificing elegance. Clothing was practical, purposeful, and yet aesthetically refined.

An interesting fact here is that Indus Valley styling was so influential that elements of it travelled far beyond the subcontinent. Scholars such as Jonathan Mark Kenoyer have observed that the headdress discovered in the royal cemetery of Ur in ancient Mesopotamia may have been imported from the Indus Valley

Civilisation. This stands as a testament to the far-reaching appeal and enduring excellence of Indian craftsmanship.

While a wide variety of garments existed, the most common attire in ancient India consisted of two principal pieces. The *antariya* covered the lower body and was tied at the waist with a knot or secured with a band of cloth, leather, or metal functioning like a belt. It could be knee-length or ankle-length, skirt-like or dhoti-like, light and translucent or heavy and richly embroidered. Complementing it was the *uttariya*, a rectangular cloth draped over one or both shoulders, covering the back partially or fully.

The common folk typically wore simple, lightweight uttariyas or dispensed with them altogether, since much of their work was outdoors. However, the affluent adorned themselves with elaborately embroidered uttariyas draped gracefully over one shoulder, signalling prosperity and refinement. This two-piece attire often left the torso bare and the legs free, ideally suited to India's climate. As for children, practicality and freedom of movement guided their attire. Their clothing was minimal, often consisting of simple loincloths that allowed their growing bodies to move freely and remain unrestricted.

Notably, daily attire in ancient India was largely ungendered; both men and women wore variations of these garments. At times, women used an additional cloth called the *stanapatta*, tied around the chest for coverage. Interestingly, some men also wore it in an X-like pattern across the torso. In colder seasons, a garment known as the *pravara* was worn by both sexes, differing only in size.

This fluidity in dress gradually gave rise to garments that would endure across millennia. Among the most enduring of these is the saree, or shatika, which originated in ancient India and is perhaps one of the oldest surviving garments still in use today. In earlier times, the shatika was worn by both men and women, draped in diverse styles. This single, continuous length of cloth was so versatile that it inspired adaptations in other ancient cultures, including Greece. Its simplicity and adaptability made it universally appealing.

Takeaways from the Ancient Past

- In an age when fashion is often dictated by fleeting trends and influencers—frequently at the cost of comfort and lifestyle—it may be time to revisit ancient India's sartorial wisdom. Clothing can be chosen based on climate, personal constitution, profession, and ease, without sacrificing elegance.
- As the modern world strives towards eco-friendly fashion, ancient India already offers a rich repository of sustainable, nature-aligned textile traditions. These time-tested methods can be thoughtfully adapted even within our contemporary, fast-paced lives.
- The practice of cleansing undergarments in herb-infused water before drying them may still serve as a simple and effective method to maintain hygiene and promote intimate health.
- Viewing clothing as a sacred protector of both body and spirit fosters mindful consumption. In an era of excessive shopping and overindulgence, this perspective encourages us to buy thoughtfully and preserve carefully.

Chapter 4

FOOD AND CULTURE

'From earth, herbs; from herbs, food; from food, seed; and from seed, human beings. We thus consist of the essence of food.'
—Taittiriya Upanishad

Bhojanam: Food Culture in Ancient India

The purpose of tracing 11,000 years of culinary history in the Indian subcontinent is not merely to look back with nostalgia but to discern how we might return, consciously and deliberately, to a more mindful way of nourishing ourselves. And to appreciate the depth and sophistication of ancient Indian food culture, it is essential first to understand how dietary patterns were conceived and classified, for it was through these frameworks that food was woven into a larger philosophy of life.

Foundational Indian texts describe human nature through three base qualities, or *trigunas*, and it is the combination of these traits that determines an individual's temperament and suitability for different professions. The three gunas are *sattva*, *rajas*, and *tamas*. Sattva imparts higher intelligence, a quest for knowledge, and spiritual inclination. Rajas is associated with passion, desire, enthusiasm, movement, and dynamism, while tamas signifies inertia, illusion, materiality, and a sense of heaviness.

These qualities also found expression in food. In dietary terms, they translated into calming and gentle foods, spicy and high-energy foods, and heavy or predominantly carnivorous diets respectively. The gastronomic experts of ancient India meticulously identified food varieties and recipes suited to every combination of personality traits and professions. Yogis and ascetics, whose lives were devoted to inner inquiry, consumed a single simple meal a day, consisting largely of natural and uncooked foods such as fruits and legumes, so that even the craving for food would not distract them from their truth-seeking pursuits.

Priests, engaged in rituals and pious activities, followed a pure vegetarian diet with the most subtle flavour profiles. Such food cultivated calmness, patience, and sustained focus, qualities essential for performing rituals that lasted hours, chanting mantras for long periods, and remaining detached from material pleasures. Kshatriyas—kings and warriors—on the other hand, consumed a well-balanced diet that included meat, fruits, dairy, cereals, and pulses. Their roles demanded physical strength, agility, endurance, and resilience, all of which were supported through carefully planned meals.

Ancient medical texts such as *Ashtanga Hridayam*, *Charaka Samhita*, and *Sushruta Samhita* went even further, providing detailed dietary guidelines for children of different ages, pregnant women, senior citizens, and those suffering from specific diseases. Ayurveda generally discouraged food consumption after sunset, except under particular conditions. Thousands of years before concepts like the paleo diet, keto diet, or intermittent fasting became fashionable, ancient India had already developed a sophisticated dietary system that customised food based on personality, profession, age, and health.

This dietary sophistication was neither incidental nor isolated; it emerged from a deeply rooted healing tradition.

In Ayurveda, food is regarded as the foremost pillar of life, alongside sleep and *brahmacharya* (the disciplined pursuit of ultimate truth). An ancient Sanskrit dictum states, 'When the diet is pure, the mind is pure,' highlighting the intimate connection between nourishment and consciousness. Accordingly, diet occupies a central place in Ayurvedic healing. The concept of *pathya vyavastha* prescribes specific foods for particular ailments, clearly distinguishing what should be consumed from what must be avoided. Through such mindful selection and disciplined practice, Ayurveda sought not merely to eliminate disease but to cultivate harmony across body, mind, and spirit.

A similar holistic approach to eating is found in the *Charaka Samhita*, written over 2,600 years ago, which states, 'Without a proper diet, medicines are of no use; with a proper diet, medicines are unnecessary.' It is therefore not surprising that ancient Indians selected ingredients from nature and combined them as though preparing medicinal formulations to sustain health. They also precisely measured the quantity of each ingredient and component, much like determining the dosage of a remedy.

Thus, we can see how the holistic and mindful food culture of ancient India seamlessly blended a personalised approach with spiritual and yogic disciplines, shaping eating habits that supported healthy, active, and long lives. And today, when lifestyle- and food-related disorders are increasingly prevalent, this holistic approach to eating is more relevant than ever. Revisiting the ancient Indian understanding of food may offer one of the simplest yet most effective paths to lasting health.

Hearth to Heart: The Ritual Art of Cooking and Eating

Continuing from the rhythms of the morning—the purifying bath and the donning of fresh garments—the ancient Indians would then prepare to partake of the day's first meal. Having invoked the principles of earth, sky, water, and air, they now invoked fire. This was the time to kindle the outer flame so that it could nourish the inner one—the sacred fire within the belly. Cooking, therefore, was not merely a domestic act; it was an elemental dialogue between the outer and the inner worlds.

The notable point here is that, for the ancient Indians, food carried a deeper philosophical meaning. It was never merely fuel to appease hunger or sustenance to energise the body, but a way of life and a powerful means of shaping personality. The *Brihadaranyaka Upanishad* declares, 'Food and the eater—that is the extent of the whole world.' For this reason, generations devoted themselves to refining their meals, ensuring that food nourished not only the body but also the mind.

This reverence naturally shaped the manner in which food was prepared and the space in which it was cooked. Food was accorded divine status, and the kitchen itself was revered as a sacred space. A Sanskrit verse proclaims: 'Food is Brahma, taste is Vishnu, and digestion is a divine process. When consumed with devotion, it brings satisfaction.' It is therefore no surprise that kitchens were often located adjacent to the puja room. Such sanctity was upheld not merely in belief but through disciplined daily conduct. Thus, one entered the kitchen only after an early morning bath and a change into fresh clothes. Once cooking began, the cook did not leave the space until the process was complete. And if one stepped out midway, purification was required before re-entering. These disciplines ensured not only ritual sanctity but also the highest standards of hygiene.

Another customary practice was to chant the Annapoorna mantra before cooking began, invoking the goddess of nourishment. This ritual reinforced the sanctity of food, the importance of preparing it mindfully, and the responsibility of avoiding waste. The sun and the planetary forces were also invoked not out of superstition but as a subtle acknowledgement of the cosmic forces that sustain agricultural life. By intertwining faith with sustainability, the people of ancient India ensured that reverence would safeguard ecological balance. They understood the importance of protecting the atmosphere and using food resources judiciously, embedding environmental consciousness within daily rituals.

This spirit of reverence extended beyond the kitchen into the very act of eating. Before a meal, the ancient Indians would wash their hands, feet, and mouth, preparing themselves both physically and mentally. They then sat on the floor and offered prayers to Mother Nature in gratitude for the food, seeking the well-being of every natural element that had contributed to it. They also prayed for the health and prosperity of the person who had prepared the meal.

Additionally, meals were often served on leaves such as plantain (banana) or lotus leaves. Banana leaves, rich in polyphenols, are believed to help prevent several lifestyle disorders. Serving food on fresh leaves also ensured hygiene, as it eliminated the risk of contamination through reuse.

It should also be noted that the entire process of eating was never rushed but was instead approached and regarded as a complete sensory experience. The sight of the food, the subtle sounds while eating, its enticing aroma, the richness of taste, and the tactile sensation of touching it with the hand and feeling it in the mouth together made the act intimate and holistic.

In this way, eating was elevated from a mere biological necessity and mechanical act into a conscious expression of gratitude and awareness. It became a daily reminder that nourishment sustains not only the body, but also the senses and the spirit.

From Barley to Biryani: The Foundations of Ancient Indian Cuisine

As we have seen, the ancient Indians truly believed that you are what you eat, and this conviction was reflected in the recipes they prepared. Among the earliest and most noteworthy of these was *Apupa*, a form of sweet cake that is mentioned repeatedly in Vedic literature. Made from barley flour, the loose dough was flattened into cakes and fried in ghee, then dipped in honey to sweeten and soften them before serving. This delicacy, with minor variations, survives to this day in the form of *malpua*. Additionally, pulverised barley known as *saktu*, a porridge made by boiling barley in milk called *odana*, and *karambha*, a dish combining barley and yoghurt, are also referenced in the Vedas.

The ingredients chosen for these recipes reveal a broader picture of the staples and produce that sustained ancient Indian diets. One of the earliest staple grains was barley, known as *yava* in Sanskrit, which appears frequently in the *Rigveda*. Archaeological evidence suggests that it was in use long before the Vedic period, highlighting its importance as a principal grain. Millets formed another dietary cornerstone, alongside pulses such as chickpeas, red lentils, and green peas. The four Vedas reference an array of fruits and vegetables—*bael* fruit (*Aegle marmelos*), mangoes, jujubes, water chestnuts, dates, lotus stalks, roots, and gourds, among many others.

Ancient Indians also consumed a wide variety of drinks to quench their thirst. Water was stored in earthen pots, which kept it cool, clean, and naturally filtered. Drinking water was often infused with potent herbs such as *tulasi* (*Ocimum sanctum*) and *pathimukham* (*Biancaea sappan*). Milk, too, held an important place in the daily diet, while buttermilk mixed with fresh green herbs was commonly consumed for its cooling and digestive properties.

Moreover, dairy products—milk, yoghurt, butter, ghee, and cream—were consumed in varied forms. Honey served as the primary sweetener in desserts, while jaggery entered the culinary repertoire during the Vedic era. The ancient Indian diet was thus wholesome, natural, and deeply aligned with seasonal and ecological rhythms.

Beyond grains and dairy, another defining feature of this culinary tradition was its mastery of spices. As early as 3,000 BCE, ancient Indians were already adept at cultivating black pepper, turmeric, mustard, and cardamom, enriching their cuisine with both flavour and medicinal value. Archaeological discoveries further reveal that merchants of the Indus Valley were exporting spices—including clove heads—to Ur in Mesopotamia as early as 2,350 BCE, indicating not only agricultural sophistication but also active participation in long-distance trade.

Notably, in 2010, the University of Vancouver conducted a starch grain analysis on a cooking pot discovered at a burial site in Farmana, Haryana, dating back over 4,000 years to the Harappan civilisation. The analysis revealed traces of brinjal (eggplant), turmeric, ginger, and garlic. Based on the site's location, researchers also concluded that salt was used in the dish, as ancient Indians had been extracting salt for more than 4,500 years. This Harappan evidence arguably points to the oldest recorded curry in human history. Archaeological and historical records further suggest that the globally popular dish *biryani* originated in India. Ancient texts such as the Ramayana mention a preparation called *mamsodana*, in which rice and meat are cooked together, reinforcing this claim. It is important to recognise that all these material records represent only a fraction of the story. One can only imagine how many additional centuries of gastronomic wisdom lie buried beneath the soil of this ancient land, which is one of the earliest cradles of food civilisation.

In summary, within ancient Indian society, every aspect of eating—from what to eat and how to eat, to who should eat which foods—was approached with care and deliberation. Eating was regarded as a conscious act, a dialogue between the body and food, and between the individual and nature.

Takeaways from the Ancient Past

- Expressing gratitude before cooking and eating fosters humility and serves as a gentle reminder that we share the intricate food chain with countless other beings.
- Viewing food as 'the tastiest medicine to avoid other medicines' encourages moderation and offers a simple solution to overeating and obesity.
- Considering food as divine or sacred ensures its judicious use and helps prevent wastage, a serious issue in many parts of the world today.
- Designing dietary plans based on personality and profession presents an innovative and pleasant approach to nutrition, rather than treating dieting as a burden.
- Eating at least one meal a day on a leaf can be a small yet meaningful step towards sustainability and may even inspire people to grow such plants at home.
- Treating the kitchen as a sacred space instils responsibility to use pure and unadulterated ingredients.

Chapter 5

KNOWLEDGE AND LEARNING

'Lead me from ignorance to knowledge.
Lead me from darkness to light.
Lead me from death to immortality.
Peace, peace, peace.'
—Brihadaranyaka Upanishad

Nalanda: The Glorious Centre of Knowledge and Learning

With the body nourished and the mind awakened, ancient Indians would then turn to their daily duties and professional engagements. And for the youth, that primary duty was education. Yet this education extended far beyond rote learning and was not confined to classrooms or scriptures. Instead, it was embraced as a way of life by infusing knowledge into every aspect of daily living, so seamlessly integrated that even the simplest gesture carried a deeper meaning and moral layer.

For instance, whenever someone left home for the day, they would prostrate at the feet of the elders to seek their blessings. This gesture, known in Sanskrit as *sashtanga namaskaram*—with *sa* meaning 'with,' *ashta* meaning 'eight,' *anga* meaning 'limb,' and *namaskaram* meaning 'greeting'—involves a full prostration in which eight parts of the body—the feet, knees, hands, chest, and head—touch the ground. While such daily prostrations carry physical health benefits, the ancients perceived a far deeper symbolism. By lowering oneself at the feet of an elder, one symbolically surrendered the ego. Therefore, beginning the day in this manner ensured that one acted not from pride but from humility and reverence. Put simply, in lowering the body, one elevated the self. And in today's world, where generations often drift apart and elders are sometimes seen as outdated, reviving this simple practice can help restore bonds of respect and continuity. It is but one example of how ancient India masterfully wove enduring values into everyday rituals for long-term civilisational strength.

So, if such care was taken to embed wisdom into daily domestic life, it comes as no surprise that ancient Indians were also pioneers in envisioning large-scale centres of learning. Among these, none shone more brilliantly than the celebrated Nalanda Mahavihara in the powerful kingdom of Magadha.

Nalanda was located near Rajagriha, about eleven *yojanas* (one yojana being approximately eight kilometres) from Pataliputra, in present-day Patna, Bihar. For nearly seven centuries during which it flourished, there was nothing comparable to it anywhere in the world. This monastic university predates the University of Oxford and Europe's oldest university, Bologna, by more than five hundred years, which is a testament to the intellectual foresight of ancient India.

To understand the emergence of such an advanced institution, we must look at the evolution of the Buddhist monastic tradition. The Buddha institutionalised annual retreats during the rainy season for wandering monks who had renounced worldly life. Over time, he permitted permanent abodes to be constructed for them. These dwellings, known as *viharas* or *addhayogas*, were storeyed buildings, attics, or caves designed to provide safety and an environment conducive to introspection and meditation. When these monasteries expanded in scale and scholarly stature, they came to be known as *mahaviharas* (the great monasteries). Thousands of erudite monks would reside in them, dedicating themselves to the study of Buddhist texts and the pursuit of nirvana.

Initially, these viharas were meant exclusively for monks who had renounced worldly ties. However, over time, they gradually opened their doors to students as well, who were free to return to worldly life after completing their education. It was perhaps during this transition—from exclusive monastic retreat to inclusive scholarly institution—that the earliest seeds of organised, large-scale education were sown.

It was upon this fertile foundation that the great university of Nalanda arose as a beacon of knowledge that illuminated not only India but the wider world. Founded under the patronage of King Kumaragupta I of the Gupta dynasty around the fifth century CE, Nalanda would go on to shape the trajectory of art, scholarship, and Mahayana Buddhism across the Indian subcontinent for centuries. It is also worth noting that the kingdom of Magadha itself was an ancient and thriving civilisation, with settlements dating back to at least 1,200 BCE. By the time Mahavira and the Buddha walked its sacred soil, the region already carried centuries of cultural and intellectual legacy. The very name of this institution carries layers of meaning that reflect its purpose and importance. Archaeologist Hiranand Sastri, who led the excavation of the Nalanda ruins, attributes its name to the abundance of *nālas* (lotus stalks) in the region and suggests that Nalanda may have meant 'the giver of lotus stalks.' To imagine that such a magnificent institution derived its name from a delicate botanical detail is both charming and ironic, is it not? However, a closer look at the Sanskrit roots of the word reveals a deeper insight into the significance of this name. The word may also be understood as *nalam + da*, where nalam means 'lotus'—symbol of light, knowledge, and wisdom—and da means 'to give.' Thus, Nalanda becomes 'the giver of knowledge,' or more evocatively, 'where knowledge is endlessly shared.'

From Gurukulam to Global Campus: A University Without Equal

In ancient India, education was regarded as a lifelong pursuit, and the passage from foundational learning to advanced scholarship was a milestone of profound importance. So, once basic education at the *gurukulam* was completed, a mid-teenager aspiring to higher knowledge would seek admission to the foremost universities of the land. Takshashila, Pushpagiri, Nalanda, Valabhi, Odantapuri, Vikramashila, Somapura, and Sharada Peetham were some of the oldest and the most illustrious centres of learning. Among these, securing a place at Nalanda was considered one of the greatest challenges. Each year, tens of thousands of students from across the known world arrived with hopes of entry, yet only a handful—two or three out of ten—succeeded. It was said that even the gatekeepers were accomplished scholars, and no student could enter the grand campus without first engaging them in rigorous debate. The intensity of this selection process reflected the university's dedication to nurturing not just memory but critical thinking and insight.

At the grand gates of Nalanda, pristinely dressed sentinels awaited, each adorned with tall cotton headdresses. The senior guard would enquire about the applicant's origin, purpose of visit, and credentials. Once these were presented, he would pose fundamental questions on Buddhism. This process was designed not merely to test factual knowledge but to evaluate the student's perspective, independent thinking, and philosophical depth. It is important to note that, although Nalanda imparted both Hindu and Buddhist knowledge systems, it was primarily a Buddhist institution dedicated to disseminating profound Buddhist wisdom. Therefore, it was natural that the administration sought to understand each student's intellectual disposition towards its core teachings. If the responses were satisfactory, the guard would declare in flawless Sanskrit, 'Welcome to Nalanda, where learning is the greatest joy.'

Beyond the gates awaited an experience that would remain etched in memory for a lifetime. During the Gupta period—often regarded as the Golden Age of India—the Nalanda Mahavihara flourished under royal patronage in the fifth and sixth centuries CE. Spread across vast acres, its red-brick edifices stood both imposing and elegant. Expansive lecture halls and amphitheatres accommodated thousands during assemblies, while individual classrooms could seat hundreds at a time. Students were expected to remain until lectures concluded, reflecting the discipline of the institution. Thoughtfully designed, many classrooms even housed wells to provide clean drinking water, ensuring comfort during long sessions of study.

Moreover, the campus demonstrated remarkable scientific sophistication for its time. Accounts preserved in the journals of Chinese travellers of the time suggest that Nalanda housed an astronomical observatory and included astronomy in its curriculum. Records also indicate the presence of a clepsydra, or water clock, which kept accurate time for the entire kingdom of Magadha—a remarkable testament to its scientific sophistication. The campus was also adorned with graceful shrines and monasteries where Buddhist monks and scholars lived their monastic lives in harmony with rigorous academic pursuits.

Such scientific and scholarly excellence was complemented by an equally advanced approach to student life and logistics. Nalanda, recognised as the first great residential university of its kind, welcomed students from all over the world and provided comprehensive accommodation and support. The administration spared no effort in ensuring their welfare. Dormitories rose three storeys high, containing over three hundred rooms. New and intermediate students resided on the lower floors, while advanced scholars occupied the uppermost level. Stairways connected the floors, and each student was allotted a private chamber furnished with a cot, a study table, bookshelves, storage space for personal belongings, and even a lamp for late-night study.

However, the crowning glory of Nalanda was its magnificent library, Dharmaganja, which means the 'Mountain of Truth.' This extraordinary complex comprised three grand multi-storeyed edifices: Ratnasagara (Ocean of Jewels), Ratnodadhi (Sea of Jewels), and Ratnaranjaka (The Bejewelled). Among them, Ratnodadhi rose to a staggering nine storeys, housing some of the rarest and most sacred manuscripts of the contemporary world. In an age when even modest elevations inspired awe, a nine-storeyed structure must have seemed nothing short of miraculous. It is no wonder that foreign chroniclers described it as 'the tower that kissed the clouds.'

The entire library complex is believed to have housed over nine million manuscripts, making it perhaps the largest repository of knowledge in the world at that time. Considering the sophistication of the collection and its sheer magnitude, we can reasonably infer that Nalanda employed an advanced system of classification, which was possibly inspired by the linguistic and textual frameworks developed by the great Sanskrit grammarian Panini, who lived more than a millennium before Nalanda's inception.

Such careful organisation and curation allowed the library to expand steadily while maintaining order and accessibility. Moreover, when a Buddhist scholar of Nalanda passed away, his personal manuscripts and collections were absorbed into the institutional archives. Thus, alongside the Mahavihara's official acquisitions, countless private collections enriched the shelves for nearly a thousand years, transforming Dharmaganja into a living ocean of accumulated wisdom.

Tragically, this unparalleled treasure was reduced to ashes during an arson attack by an invading army. The flames are said to have raged for months, consuming palm-leaf manuscripts and painted wooden folios that had preserved centuries of human thought. Only a handful survived, rescued by fleeing monks who carried them across borders. Some of these remnants can today be found in institutions such as the Los Angeles County Museum of Art in the United States and the Yarlung Museum in Tibet, serving as silent witnesses to a lost intellectual empire.

Thus, it becomes evident that Nalanda was not merely a university, but a living embodiment of disciplined scholarship, global exchange, and the relentless pursuit of wisdom.

Pedagogical Excellence: Curriculum, Culture, and Character

In contrast to today, where education is often treated as a commercial enterprise, Nalanda provided both instruction and accommodation completely free of charge. Maintaining such a vast and vibrant institution, however, demanded considerable support. Generous patronage came not only from kings—even those who ruled long after the Gupta dynasty—but also from influential officials, village leaders, and prosperous merchants, all of whom played a vital role in sustaining its legacy. The Chinese pilgrim Hiuen Tsang records that Nalanda received grants from more than one hundred villages. This highlights how ancient India fostered a culture in which communities took pride in investing their daily earnings to support a society grounded in knowledge and wisdom. It should also be noted that although Nalanda primarily propagated Buddhist philosophy, many of its greatest patrons were Hindu rulers and nobles, demonstrating the intellectual inclusivity of the age.

Admission to Nalanda Mahavihara was open to all, irrespective of origin. The only prerequisites were a strong foundational education and an unquenchable thirst for wisdom. Unlike modern systems where influence may overshadow merit, at the gates of Nalanda, only intellect and presence of mind prevailed.

The admission process reflected this uncompromising ethos. After the initial debate with the gatekeeper, aspirants underwent both oral and written examinations. These assessments tested their mastery of Sanskrit and the depth of their prior education. Since the majority of primary texts were composed in Sanskrit, proficiency in the language and its intricate grammar was indispensable. That said, many students faltered at the formidable oral examination, while others withdrew in recognition of the university's exacting standards. Only the truly prepared crossed its threshold, ready to immerse themselves in the boundless ocean of knowledge within.

Being primarily a religious institution, Nalanda made theology and philosophy compulsory for all its students. Yet its intellectual horizon extended far beyond doctrinal study. The curriculum embraced the major Buddhist philosophical schools along with the Vedas; *hetuvidya* (logic); *shabdavidya* (grammar and philology); *chikitsavidya* or Ayurveda (medicine), which included *shalyavidya* (surgery); potent ritualistic knowledge from the Atharvaveda; *jyotisastra* (astronomy); and Samkhya, the dualistic school of philosophy. Furthermore, students were expected to complete foundational courses in these disciplines before the age of twenty-one. However, there was no rigid duration of residence at the university. The length of study depended upon the time each student required to master a subject and, more importantly, upon the depth of his intellectual passion.

The records of the Chinese scholars Hiuen Tsang and I-Tsing illustrate this flexibility. Both studied Yogacara philosophy at Nalanda, yet Hiuen Tsang completed his education in five years, while I-Tsing remained for nearly ten. Such variation reveals that learning at Nalanda was not bound by a clock but by commitment and capability.

The breadth of subjects attracted students and scholars from China, Indonesia, Japan, Korea, Persia, Turkey, Rome, and Greece. From I-Tsing's accounts, we learn that within fifty years of Hiuen Tsang's visit, fifty-six Chinese scholars had been educated at Nalanda. Considering that only about twenty per cent of applicants secured admission, one can reasonably infer that several times that number must have journeyed to its gates in hope.

Moreover, much like the brahminical gurukulam system, Nalanda University fostered a close and personal bond between teacher and student, with a ratio of roughly one teacher to six or seven students. At its zenith, the university accommodated over 10,000 students and nearly 2,000 distinguished faculty members. Among them, Aryabhatta, revered as the father of Indian mathematics, is believed to have served as one of its leading scholars in the sixth century CE, further cementing Nalanda's unparalleled academic stature.

This favourable teacher-student ratio also enabled the institution to provide intimate mentorship and personalised guidance. The Chinese monk I-Tsing recorded in his journal, 'I used to converse with these teachers so intimately that I was able to receive invaluable instructions personally from them.' In fact, the relationship was so deep that teacher and disciple were expected to care for one another in times of illness. This has been a longstanding practice dating back to Vedic times, where the teacher regarded the disciple as a son, and the disciple revered the teacher as a father. And in an era when relationships often grow mechanical and tiresome, reviving such a culture of reverence and care could help restore a profound human dimension to education.

The administrative structure of Nalanda was strikingly democratic. Matters of governance required assembly and collective deliberation, not only among officials but also among resident monks. When an issue arose, the officer known as the Viharapala would circulate the matter and report it to each resident monk individually. If even a single monk objected, the motion would not pass. Though hierarchy existed in teaching and management, when it came to opinions and values, every voice mattered. It is astonishing to imagine a university gatekeeper who was himself a distinguished scholar, empowered to examine applicants for higher education—a scenario rare in any era of world history.

However, it is striking that there is no clear record of female students or faculty at Nalanda. This absence appears unusual for two reasons. First, the Vedas and Upanishads—compiled centuries or even millennia before Nalanda—celebrate numerous erudite women scholars such as Gargi, Maitreyi, Lopamudra, Apala, Romasha, and Vagambhrini. Second, the Buddha himself ordained women into the monastic order and ensured their education in Buddhist scriptures and philosophy. The silence surrounding women at Nalanda thus remains an intriguing historical question.

In addition, discipline at Nalanda reflected remarkable psychological insight. Corporal punishment was not practised. For minor offences, students were barred from visiting their favourite spots within the Mahavihara. This practice aligns with what modern psychology calls 'negative punishment,' where a pleasant stimulus is removed to discourage undesirable behaviour. As for repeated or serious offences, expulsion was the ultimate consequence, but only after careful evaluation and the consent of the student's personal tutor. Justice, therefore, was tempered with mentorship and discernment.

Nalanda followed the same approach of avoiding theatrics and coercion in matters concerning its faculty members. A monk who acted without unanimous consent could be required to leave the monastery. In cases of disagreement, persuasion was achieved through reasoned argument and clarity of thought, never through force. Overall, the lives of monks, scholars, and students revolved around these strict yet virtuous codes of conduct, and no one—novice or veteran—was exempt. An interesting fact is that throughout the seven centuries of the Mahavihara's existence, not a single resident deliberately violated its fundamental rules, such was the depth of discipline and collective integrity.

Nalanda also ensured that it remained intellectually current. The Mahavihara regularly compiled encyclopaedic works that gathered emerging knowledge from diverse traditions, keeping scholars abreast of contemporary developments and often ahead of their time. One such surviving work, *Tattvasangraha*, stands as testimony that Nalanda was not merely a Buddhist centre but a vibrant institution where Buddhist and non-Buddhist philosophies alike were studied, debated, and systematically preserved.

In addition to this, their curriculum was so dynamic that it evolved whenever new and relevant knowledge emerged in the world. Also, the custodians and mentors of Nalanda conceived education as a means to develop the intellectual, political, moral, spiritual, and aesthetic dimensions of the individual. The goal was not merely to secure prestigious positions in royal administrations but to cultivate men capable of leading peaceful, purposeful personal and social lives. This, of course, was in addition to the central focus of the Mahavihara—the sublime ascetic path towards renunciation and nirvana.

It is a recorded fact that Nalanda alumni were highly sought after in elite professional circles. I-Tsing notes in his journals that monks from Nalanda found it remarkably easy to secure high-ranking positions in foreign royal courts simply by presenting their Nalanda diplomas. The tangible value of graduating from such an illustrious institution is further revealed by the discovery of forged 'Nalanda diplomas' by archaeologists. These counterfeit certificates were so skilfully made that they could deceive the untrained eye. This points to two conclusions: first, that job fraud is hardly a modern invention; and second, that the reputation of this great university commanded extraordinary respect across lands.

Furthermore, Nalanda was not insular. The university regularly sent its most accomplished scholars to lands such as China, Korea, Japan, Indonesia, and Sri Lanka to propagate Buddhist philosophy and teachings. This ancient network of intellectual exchange profoundly shaped the course of Buddhism across Asia and established Nalanda as a luminous centre of global learning long before the modern idea of international academia emerged.

Yet knowledge, then as now, was power. It is therefore unsurprising that Nalanda became a target for invading forces. As the intellectual pride of the land, it symbolised cultural strength, and to strike it was to wound the spirit of a civilisation. Though the Mahavihara suffered attacks across centuries, it is widely believed that the final devastating blow came around 1,200 CE under Muhammad Bakhtiyar Khilji. However, evidence suggests that the institution lingered on for some time before eventually fading into the tides of history.

If there is one lesson the modern world could reclaim from ancient India's educational system, it is this relentless emphasis on moulding individuals who are true seekers of knowledge, preservers of human values, and seers who perceive life as an interconnected whole, rather than competitive professionals trained to function within the narrow boundaries of their expertise. Especially today, when higher education often confines itself to narrow specialisation, this holistic and well-rounded approach becomes all the more important.

Learning as a Way of Life: Wisdom at the Heart of Education

As outlined above, in ancient India, education was regarded as a profound journey towards becoming the best version of oneself. It extended far beyond the technical acquisition of knowledge and skills and was considered as a path of holistic development aimed at realising the truth about the self and the world. Therefore, learning was not fragmented into isolated competencies but woven into a larger inquiry into meaning, purpose, and inner refinement.

Within this vision, educational institutions functioned as largely meritocratic and egalitarian spaces where students were not meant to receive special treatment on the basis of social, economic, or political status but were instead evaluated on the basis of their aptitude, discipline, and commitment to learning. Education was also considered incomplete without an understanding of one's culture and heritage, for every individual was seen as the evolutionary expression of a civilisation. To know oneself fully required knowing the traditions, philosophies, stories, and intellectual inheritances that shaped one's collective past. Hence, great importance was placed on engaging deeply with the many dimensions of India's rich civilisational legacy.

In summary, the central message of ancient India's educational ethos was that education is not merely a means to employment, social mobility, or personal advancement; it is a way of life. This leads us on a journey both inward and outward, discovering oneself through inquiry, understanding the cosmos through contemplation, and discerning one's purpose by recognising the subtle bond between the individual and the universe. And in nurturing this intimate and enduring connection, true wisdom arises.

Such an understanding of education naturally prompts us to reflect on its relevance in our own times. In today's contemporary world, while globalisation has brought undeniable opportunities, it has also contributed to the gradual erosion of cultural distinctiveness. In such a context, thoughtfully introducing elements of ancient Indian wisdom, even as optional subjects from the primary level, could be a meaningful step. Foundational Indian philosophy, folklore, and ancient history would not serve as instruments of nostalgia but as anchors of identity. Early exposure to these streams of thought could instil in the next generation a deeper understanding of what it means to belong to an ancient civilisation and awaken in them the curiosity to explore their roots further. Over time, this would become not merely a pedagogical choice but a cultural safeguard, preserving values that have endured for millennia.

Takeaways from the Ancient Past

- Education is not a means of following an already paved path in order to become professionally successful. Rather, it is about paving one's own path through the process of discovering oneself and one's purpose in the world and in life.
- It is important to recognise that education is not merely the acquisition of knowledge and enhancement of skills, but a holistic development aimed at realising one's material as well as spiritual potential.
- The guru-shishya (teacher-student) relationship should not be merely professional, but rooted in love, respect, and a shared responsibility to care for and nurture one another.
- Education should never be considered a business, but rather a collective responsibility of society directed towards the all-encompassing development of the individual.

Chapter 6

HEALTH AND AYURVEDA

'As is the microcosm, so is the macrocosm.'
—Charaka Samhita

Ayurveda: The Tradition of Holistic Healthcare

Ancient Indians belonged to a remarkably advanced civilisation in which the wellness of the people was a top priority. It is therefore natural that they aspired to a high standard of living and gave utmost importance to medicine and healthcare. In fact, India was perhaps one of the earliest cultures to develop a mature medical system. Excavations from various sites suggest that medical procedures such as dentistry and trepanation were practised as early as the Indus Valley period. One of the earliest reliable pieces of evidence of systematic medicine and trained medical practitioners in India dates back to around 3,500 years ago, during the Vedic period.

This early commitment to healthcare was deeply intertwined with a broader understanding of life and nature. Vedic literature underscores that the balance of the entire ecosystem is essential for maintaining the health and longevity of the individual. For this reason, ancient Indians relied extensively on nature and on herbs sourced from the natural world for healthcare. The Rigveda declares, 'For a knowledgeable healer, the herbs rally together akin to an army of kings.' The Vedas also mention several sages and schools of herbalists who identified, described, and popularised the medicinal use of specific plants. Additionally, a plant was often named after the sage who discovered and studied it. For instance, sage Kanva was credited with identifying the medicinal properties of a plant called *apamarga*, which subsequently came to be known as the Kanva plant. Is it not fascinating that thousands of years before modern biology formalised such practices, ancient Indians associated the discoverer's name with botanical nomenclature?

Coming back to our earlier discussion on healthcare in ancient India, the branch of knowledge that dealt with health and disease was called Ayurveda. *Ayu* means 'life' or 'lifespan,' and *veda* means 'profound knowledge.' Thus, Ayurveda literally translates to 'the profound knowledge of life.' Since it originated several millennia ago, one might assume that it was an archaic system of healing. But consider the eight branches of Ayurveda that were systematically practised by those remarkable researchers of life:

1. *Kaya chikitsa* (general medicine)
2. *Bala chikitsa* (paediatrics)
3. *Graha chikitsa* (psychiatry)
4. *Urdhvanga chikitsa* (relating to diseases of the head and neck, including the ears, nose, throat, and eyes)
5. *Shalya chikitsa* (surgery)
6. *Damshtra chikitsa* (toxicology)
7. *Jara chikitsa* (geriatrics)
8. *Vrishya chikitsa* (treatment of sexual dysfunctions and infertility)

These eight divisions were collectively known as the *ashtanga*, or the eight limbs, of Ayurveda.

At the core of Ayurveda lies the doctrine of *tridosha*, the theory of the three humours. Ancient practitioners believed that health depended upon the delicate balance of *vata*, *pitta*, and *kapha*, and that their imbalance resulted in disease. These are often translated into English as wind, bile, and phlegm, simply for lack of more precise equivalents. In truth, the tridoshas are far more nuanced concepts, layered with meanings that extend beyond these approximate translations and carry deeper significance for ancient physicians.

We cannot proceed further without speaking of two of the greatest pioneers of Ayurveda from ancient India. Sushruta, who lived between 700 and 600 BCE, is revered as the father of surgery. His monumental work, the *Sushruta Samhita*, is an astonishingly detailed treatise on surgical procedures that were aeons ahead of their time. He classified surgery into eight principal categories: *chedya* (excision), *lekhya* (scarification), *vedhya* (puncturing), *esya* (exploration), *ahrya* (extraction), *visraya* (evacuation), and *sivya* (suturing). In his text, he describes in remarkable detail the ophthalmologic procedure for the ejection of cataract. Even more astonishing is the fact that Sushruta performed reconstructive plastic surgeries. His T-flap technique of rhinoplasty, or nose reconstruction, continues to influence surgical methods across the world to this day.

Equally towering in stature was Charaka, a physician, researcher, and author of the celebrated *Charaka Samhita*. This elaborate work, composed in eight volumes and extending over 120 chapters, systematically presents the general principles of healthy living, pathology, anatomy, prognosis based on sense organs, therapeutics, pharmaceutics and toxicology, nutrition and dietetics, sexual health, and indicators of successful treatment. Charaka identified, classified, and described the medicinal properties of hundreds of plants and trees in his remarkable compendium. Together, the *Ashtanga Hridayam*, *Sushruta Samhita*, and *Charaka Samhita* form the *Brhat Trayi*, or the Great Triad of Ayurvedic compositions. These texts drew their inspiration and foundational knowledge from the ancient Vedic corpus, especially the *Atharva Veda*.

Despite being an elaborate, specialised, and highly developed system, Ayurveda strongly advocated a prophylactic philosophy centred on lifestyle regulation to prevent disease. Ancient Indians observed that the human body is at its weakest during the *varsha ritu*, the monsoon season from mid-July to mid-September, when digestion and overall vitality decline and susceptibility to illness increases. Accordingly, they prescribed a specially designed medicated diet rich in herbs and moderate in spices during this period. The texts also advised adopting a relatively austere lifestyle at this time, withdrawing from indulgences and engaging more deeply in spiritual practices. Such discipline was intended not only to shield the body from pathogens and lifestyle disorders but also to fortify the mind for another year of active living.

It is also worth noting that Ayurveda consistently emphasised the intricate relationship between body and mind. The ancient texts declared that to pursue the four ultimate aims of life—righteousness, prosperity, desire, and self-realisation—one must first secure a long and healthy life. This, they affirmed, could be achieved through the disciplined study and practice of Ayurveda. In other words, its primary purpose was not merely the treatment of disease but the establishment of a way of life that ensured health and longevity. And when illness did arise, Ayurveda adopted a holistic approach, creating the most favourable internal and external conditions for recovery.

All these aspects highlight that in the realm of healthcare, ancient Indians were not merely pioneers but true visionaries who were far ahead of their time.

Healer and Scholar: The Expansive Role of the Vaidya

The physician in ancient India was called a *vaidya*, meaning one who possessed profound knowledge of life. Unlike many modern practitioners, the vaidya was not merely a diagnostician and healer but also a researcher, botanist, pharmacologist, and counsellor. Their role extended beyond the treatment of symptoms to understanding the patient's constitution, lifestyle, and environment, for health was seen as a delicate balance rather than the mere absence of disease.

This holistic understanding of health naturally shaped the varied roles and settings in which the vaidya practised. There were vaidyas who worked as independent practitioners and maintained their own medical facilities, as well as vaidyas employed by the state. There also existed a tradition of wandering physicians known as *charana vaidyas*, who travelled on foot seeking patients in towns and villages. There were also visiting vaidyas who attended patients in their homes upon request. In addition to this, state-sponsored medical facilities offered treatment free of charge, whereas private establishments levied fees. The state-appointed vaidyas were responsible for the health of the royal family, courtiers, and palace residents. The highest medical office in the kingdom was that of the *raja vaidya*, the chief royal physician who personally attended to the king. Also, physicians, surgeons, and toxicologists were permanently employed in the army, serving both in times of war and peace.

Equally important is the fact that medical professionals were subject to regular and rigorous scrutiny to ensure authenticity and competence. A state-issued license was mandatory before one could begin medical practice. Patients who suffered from incorrect treatment had the right to seek justice in a court of law. Although fines were imposed for malpractice, vaidyas enjoyed sufficient autonomy to explore and refine their own therapeutic approaches. Legitimate practitioners openly criticised quacks, and the state actively attempted to curb their proliferation by standardising medical education. Notably, Sushruta himself explicitly attributed the rise of quackery to inefficiency on the part of the state.

It is difficult to determine with certainty the extent to which women participated in the medical profession in those times. Interestingly, an ancient Arabic text refers to a female Indian practitioner named Rusa, whose Ayurvedic treatise was translated into Arabic by order of a Caliph of the Abbasid Empire. This reference suggests that Indian medical knowledge, and possibly women practitioners, commanded respect even beyond the subcontinent.

What stands out here is that the vaidya examined the individual as a whole, not merely the disease. He carefully assessed the patient's morphology, anatomy, and physiology; his personality and mental state; his lifestyle, including domestic environment, dietary habits, profession, and hobbies; as well as contextual factors such as time, place, and season in which the disease manifested.

Once a diagnosis was reached, treatment extended beyond medicines. It included dietary planning, lifestyle modifications, and practices aimed at improving the patient's mental well-being. In this holistic framework, yoga also played a vital role. The guiding belief was clear: 'He who practices medicine without understanding the mind of the person is not a physician but a fool.' Moreover, no two patients were treated in exactly the same way, for Ayurveda regarded every individual as unique, each with a distinct constitution and a unique interaction with the world. Thus, we can see how healthcare and disease management in ancient India were deeply personalised, holistic, and individualised.

Beyond Cure: Health as a Way of Life

As we have seen, the ancient Indians viewed health and healthcare as a lifelong discipline rooted in conscious living. Treatment was never confined to the disease alone; it centred on the total well-being of the individual who experienced it. The body, mind, habits, environment, and inner disposition were all taken into account, for illness was understood as a disturbance in an interconnected system rather than an isolated malfunction.

Modern medicine today acknowledges that even the simplest ailment may arise from multiple causes and produce varied physical and psychological effects. In this respect, the ancient Indian healthcare framework appears strikingly prescient. Its systems, particularly Ayurveda, devised treatment plans according to an individual's constitution and personality type, recognising that no two bodies or temperaments are identical. In a world increasingly drawn towards organic food, mindful routines, and preventive care, it is worth remembering that such principles were carefully observed, practised, and documented in India thousands of years ago.

This is not to diminish the immense contributions of allopathic medicine, which continues to perform extraordinary feats in diagnosing and treating complex and severe conditions. Rather, Ayurveda can be viewed as a complementary and powerful prophylactic system, one whose primary strength lies in prevention and in cultivating balance before disease takes root. Its emphasis is not merely on curing illness but on sustaining harmony in everyday life.

Importantly, adopting an Ayurvedic lifestyle need not be daunting or rigid. It can begin with small, practical steps: incorporating one Ayurveda-recommended meal into the daily routine, dedicating one day each week to eating in accordance with Ayurvedic principles, or even observing an Ayurvedic diet and lifestyle for a month each year as a conscious reset for the body and mind. Such gradual integration makes the wisdom accessible rather than overwhelming.

Today, millions from across the world travel to India seeking the benefits of the Ayurvedic way of life. In that light, it is important to reflect on a simple question: if this knowledge is part of our own civilisational inheritance, why should we overlook a system of well-being that is both accessible and deeply rooted in our tradition?

Takeaways from the Ancient Past

- Approaching health as a way of life in harmony with nature, rather than thinking about it only when one becomes unhealthy or sick, is the best way to ensure a long and balanced life.
- Focusing on the person who is suffering from the disease, rather than concentrating solely on the disease itself, ensures that treatment is customised and optimised for each individual.
- Along with treating the body, the ancient emphasis on mental wellness and the incorporation of yoga into treatment plans is a model that can be emulated even today, regardless of the system of medicine one follows.
- By sourcing medicines from nature, our ancestors not only ensured sustainability but also sought to minimise side effects as much as possible. It is perhaps time we reconsider such an approach.

Chapter 7

THE FEMININE AND CYCLES

'The way a powerful river breaks even the strongest rocks and hills, so an intelligent woman destroys the fraud propagated by the perverted. May we bow to such intelligent women.'

—Rigveda

Rajasvala: The Menstruating Feminine

When a culture envisions a good life for its people, that vision would be incomplete if it did not thoughtfully accommodate the unique biological and emotional realities of women.

The famous verse from the Sanskrit text *Manusmriti* declares:

'Yatra naaryastu pujyante
Ramante tatra devataaha.'

(Where women are respected, there the gods reside.)

This sensitivity to the intimate rhythms of a woman's life was an integral part of ancient Indian society, where womanhood was revered, and the female capacity to create new life was deeply honoured. Menarche, therefore, was not treated as an embarrassment but as a celebration. It was seen as the first visible sign of a young girl's creative potential. When she bled for the first time, the day was considered auspicious, and women from the extended family and neighbourhood gathered to bless her.

Beyond this, in many traditional households, there existed a living quarter detached from the main building, where menstruating women stayed for the first seven days of their cycle. No men or young children were allowed in that space. When a girl experienced her first menstruation, she was ceremonially welcomed into this exclusive inner circle of adult women. In a symbolic sense, it was a coming-of-age initiation into a sacred sisterhood. She was bathed, cleansed, gently padded with a soft cloth, adorned beautifully, and treated almost like a goddess. Adult women visited her, offered gifts, and the eldest female member of the family explained the physical and emotional changes she would experience. It was education wrapped in affection and dignity.

At first glance, the custom of asking menstruating women to stay away from the main house, kitchen, or prayer room appears to stem from the idea of ritual impurity. However, for a civilisation that placed such emphasis on knowledge and systematic observation, there was likely a more practical reasoning beneath the surface.

Ancient Indian knowledge systems also invested significant thought into female fertility and reproductive health. In Sanskrit, a menstruating woman is called *rajasvala*. Ayurvedic texts lay out a detailed regimen called *rajasvala paricharya*, outlining how a woman should care for herself during menstruation to preserve and strengthen fertility. This guidance includes specific dos and don'ts relating to *aahaara* (diet), *vihaara* (lifestyle), and *maanasika* (mental and emotional well-being), especially during the first three days of the cycle. The duration could be extended depending on individual variations.

Additionally, ancient Ayurvedic texts repeatedly prescribe complete rest during menstruation. This was an important consideration, as daily life in traditional households was physically demanding. This included morning and evening prayers that required elaborate preparation, such as cleaning brass, bronze, or silver lamps and utensils, plucking flowers, preparing garlands, drawing water, and scrubbing floors. Kitchen work was equally strenuous, involving grinding grains on stone slabs, pounding spices, fetching water and firewood, tending to wood-fired stoves, and preparing multiple fresh meals each day. By declaring that a menstruating woman should remain in a separate quarter, society effectively relieved her of these physically demanding responsibilities. Thus, what may appear restrictive through a modern lens may, in its original context, have functioned as a protective and restorative measure.

Beyond physical relief, it also created a distinct feminine space within the home. Moreover, within joint families where multiple women were often menstruating at the same time, this separate living space became a quiet sanctuary that was free from domestic pressures and from the constant presence of men, allowing them to rest, converse, and engage in light recreation. This area was regularly cleaned with herb-infused water and fumigated with substances like frankincense, creating what one might describe as a carefully maintained hygienic retreat. In many ways, it was designed as a sterile haven for fertile women.

Ayurveda also prescribes abstinence from sexual intercourse during menstruation, advising the woman to observe a period of brahmacharya at that time. Contemporary medical understanding now acknowledges that sexual intercourse during menstruation can increase the risk of certain infections. Some modern studies have also indicated correlations between frequent intercourse during menstruation and a higher incidence of conditions such as endometriosis among infertility patients.

All these practices and approaches, which extended beyond mere ritual or symbolism, make it evident that ancient Indian customs surrounding menstruation reflected an effort to protect, honour, and care for women's health through structured rest, hygiene, and community support.

Sacred Cycles: Diet and Discipline during Menses

Food, in the ancient Indian worldview, was never separated from physiology or well-being. Even during menstruation, dietary choices were thoughtfully prescribed to support the body's natural rhythms and recovery.

Accordingly, special care was taken to align the diet of a menstruating woman with her body's changing needs during this time. She was generally advised to follow *havishya bhojana*, which translates as the consumption of havishya, a simple and soothing diet. This included *shali* (a variety of rice), *ghrita* (clarified butter), *takra* (buttermilk), *yava* (barley), and similar wholesome foods. Ancient texts describe these foods as gentle, cooling, and restorative, capable of soothing the body and strengthening reproductive vitality. Modern research allows us to appreciate the wisdom behind these choices. Barley is known to support bowel health, improve metabolic balance, and even aid wound healing. *Shashtika shali* rice is believed to enhance nitric oxide levels, thereby improving uterine blood flow. Studies today also confirm that dairy consumption can play a stabilising role in female reproductive health, particularly in addressing hormonal imbalances.

It was further recommended that meals during menses be eaten from clay bowls and plates. We now understand that clay possesses alkaline properties that help maintain pH balance in food. Additionally, clay mixed with water and left to incubate has demonstrated bactericidal properties. Thus, what may appear ritualistic at first glance reveals a subtle interplay of hygiene, nutrition, and physiological sensitivity.

At the same time, rajasvalas were advised to avoid *teekshna* (pungent), *ushna* (excessively hot), *amala* (sour), and *lavana* (salty) foods. Meals were to be mildly flavoured and easy to digest, with generous inclusion of fruits and vegetables. The emphasis was on reducing internal irritation and metabolic strain during a phase when the body was already engaged in a natural cleansing process.

This mindful moderation extended beyond diet to other aspects of daily routine as well. Daily head-bathing was a firmly established ritual in ancient India, and menstruating women were given autonomy in this matter. It was believed that the lowering of body temperature during a head bath could trigger uterine cramps in some women or influence hormonal balance. Therefore, the decision was left to the rajasvala herself, based on her personal experience of her cycle. She was encouraged to avoid overexertion and also discouraged from sleeping during the day, so that nighttime rest remained uninterrupted and the biological clock—and thereby hormonal rhythm—remained undisturbed.

Equally significant was the emphasis on mental well-being. The rajasvala was encouraged to be *kalyanadayini*, meaning that she was to dwell on pleasant and uplifting thoughts. One hardly needs scientific validation to recognise how crucial emotional calmness is during menstruation. By removing women from the daily stresses of domestic life and placing them in a serene environment, ancient Indian households sought to create a space of psychological comfort. Women often engaged in music, light games, chanting, and gentle conversations. This was not isolation in its original spirit, but intentional retreat.

In contrast, modern society largely adopts a reactive approach. Menstrual concerns are often addressed only after symptoms become distressing, through medication or symptomatic relief. Ancient Indians, however, adopted a prophylactic framework. They structured an entire lifestyle regimen around menstruation to prevent imbalance before it manifested as disease. Remarkably, this regimen addressed not only physiological needs but also emotional and psychological stability—an approach that still feels progressive. Taken together, these points show that by weaving structured rest into the rhythm of life, ancient Indian civilisation transformed menstruation from a phase of discomfort into a period of restoration. This makes it worthwhile to revisit such simple and practical measures and consider how they might help women today experience their menstrual phase with greater ease and harmony.

Sacred Sensitivity: Ancient Practices for Modern Menstrual Well-Being

Ancient Indians understood that menstruation is a time of heightened physical and emotional sensitivity. This period assumed special significance, as fertility was not viewed merely as a biological function but was revered as a sacred creative energy. Accordingly, meticulous daily routines were prescribed to safeguard and nourish this potency.

However, in a world where the relentless pace of contemporary life often makes true rest elusive, it becomes especially important to consider how the spirit of rajasvala paricharya can be meaningfully adapted today. Residential communities could design quiet wellness spaces where women may choose to retreat briefly. Individually, women can adopt dietary moderation, intentional rest, and mental calm during this time. The essence of the practice lies not in rigid replication but in reclaiming menstruation as a time for conscious slowing down. And in doing so, the modern woman can draw inspiration from her ancient counterpart by transforming a monthly biological event into a ritual of renewal, recuperation, and inner harmony.

Takeaways from the Ancient Past

- Creating a calm sanctuary where menstruating women can rest, rejuvenate, and be temporarily relieved from strenuous responsibilities is a way to prioritise the well-being of the person, not just the condition they experience.
- Designing a diet that minimises metabolic strain and supports reproductive health through simple, naturally sourced foods is a way to live in harmony with nature and strengthen the body sustainably.
- Giving equal importance to emotional well-being and viewing menstruation as a manifestation of creative power is a way to integrate mental wellness and mindful care into daily life.

Chapter 8

LAW AND ETHICS

'The strength of a thousand is not as powerful as the strength of one who follows dharma.'

—Mahabharata

Rta to Dharma: Law and Order in Ancient India

The ancient Indians not only held physical, mental, and spiritual life in high regard, but they also gave equal importance to ethical life. The millennia-old hymn *'Loka samasta sukhino bhavantu'* (May all beings everywhere be happy) beautifully captures how this civilisation envisioned a just and compassionate world for every form of existence. They believed in universal harmony, in the idea that every individual is ethically bound to nurture and sustain the harmonious bond that connects all beings.

Underlying such an approach to life was a unifying concept that gave coherence to both nature and human behaviour, and this concept was known as *rta*. Mentioned in the world's oldest philosophical text, the Rigveda, rta embodies the idea of cosmic and moral order. In its cosmic dimension, it explains why the celestial bodies remain in their orbits, why the sun rises unfailingly, why rivers flow, and why winds blow. Everything is what it is because rta sustains its balance. Additionally, in its moral dimension, rta is the order that enables humans, animals, plants, and even divine beings to coexist in harmony. It is both the law that regulates the universe and the ethical standard that shapes human conduct.

The ancient Indians also believed that the impulse to preserve this balance is ingrained within every particle of the cosmos, and the human being is one such particle. Each individual, therefore, owed the universe an ethical responsibility and a cosmic duty to uphold this equilibrium. It is no surprise, then, that they evolved a sophisticated system of law and governance that was remarkably advanced for its time.

Such a sense of cosmic responsibility naturally found expression in the structures that governed society. One of the clearest manifestations of this ethical worldview was India's ancient and remarkably nuanced judicial framework. There was a clear distinction between civil and criminal law. There were also elaborate provisions concerning maritime trade, industry, export and import, and taxation. A notable point is that the sources of law were manifold. The first and foremost source, known as *Sruti*, comprised the four Vedas, which addressed spiritual duties, rituals, and foundational principles. The second source consisted of the *Dharma Shastras*, whose authority stemmed from the *Smriti* literature. These included texts such as the *Manu Smriti*, *Yajnavalkya Smriti*, *Narada Smriti*, *Vishnu Smriti*, *Brihaspati Smriti*, and *Katyayana Smriti*. They elaborated on dharma, the principles of righteousness and duty. The *Artha Shastras* dealt with governance and statecraft, while the *Acharas* codified customs, traditions, and regional practices.

Subsequently, as intellectual thought evolved beyond the early Vedic period, the concept of rta gradually gave rise to the more personalised and socially embedded idea of dharma. Dharma became the guiding force of life, shaping the conduct of mortals and immortals alike. Even divine beings were believed to incur karmic consequences if they strayed from dharma. Thus, by placing gods and humans under the same moral law, the ancient Indians underscored a profound truth: righteousness is universal and non-negotiable.

Moreover, dharma was not selective, nor was it subordinate to power or privilege. It permeated both the physical and metaphysical dimensions of existence. The Upanishads declare that 'The law is the king of all monarchs,' affirming that no ruler stands above justice. The great epic Mahabharata states unequivocally that a king who fails to protect his subjects, after pledging to do so, deserves the harshest punishment. In the *Arthashastra*, Kautilya writes, 'In the happiness of his subjects lies the happiness of the king; in their welfare his welfare; what pleases him he shall not consider as good, but what pleases his people he shall consider as good.' Such assertions reveal a political philosophy in which governance was inseparable from ethical accountability.

This moral vision finds its most poignant expression in the epic Ramayana. Rama, the king of Ayodhya, loved his queen deeply and had unwavering faith in her chastity. Yet, when sections of his subjects expressed disapproval over her return after captivity, he chose to part from her. The decision shattered him personally, but he placed his duty to the people above his private happiness. For him, dharma was not an abstract ideal; it was a living obligation.

Therefore, in ancient India, ethical order was not merely a philosophical concept but a lived reality. From cosmic balance to judicial codes, from divine accountability to royal responsibility, the commitment to dharma shaped the very fabric of civilisation.

Justice, Law, and Integrity: The Ethical Foundations of Governance

Administration in ancient India was neither arbitrary nor loosely arranged, but was conceived with clarity, scale, and foresight. Governance was structured to balance local autonomy with central supervision, ensuring order across vast territories. And for the sake of efficiency and effective governance, ancient Indian kingdoms were divided into carefully structured administrative units. The *sangrahana* functioned as the administrative centre for ten villages. The *kharvatika* governed two hundred villages, the *dronamukha* oversaw four hundred, and the *sthaniya*—a fortified centre—stood at the heart of eight hundred villages. This layered system ensured that governance was both local and interconnected, allowing justice and administration to function with remarkable precision.

Every sangrahana had its own local court, each comprising three *dharmastas* (jurists) and three *amatyas* (ministers). A clear judicial hierarchy existed for the smooth conduct of legal proceedings. It began with the family court presided over by a family arbitrator, moved upward to higher courts, then to the chief justice (*pradvivaka* or *adhyaksha*), and culminated in the king's court. Minor disputes were settled at the lower levels, while grave matters ascended to the royal court. An appeal system was firmly in place, and the decision of each higher court superseded that of the one below—not merely because of authority, but because the jurists at higher levels possessed deeper knowledge and more refined expertise in the subtleties of law.

One might wonder how the king's court could stand as the highest authority in matters of knowledge. And was the king necessarily the most learned in jurisprudence? The answer lies in the structure itself. The king dispensed justice under the guidance of an accomplished council of legal scholars and advisors, individuals thoroughly versed in law and ethics. These experts were expected to be fearless and independent, tasked with safeguarding justice even against royal error. The ancient jurist Katyayana clearly states that if a judge at the king's court perceives the ruler straying from fairness, it is his solemn duty to correct him. This is not the moment for pleasing speech (*vaktavyam tat priyam natra*), but for firm admonition. And a judge who fails to warn the king is himself guilty. This was the extraordinary standard of accountability upheld in ancient India.

In fact, the legal texts extended this standard by prescribing not only ethical principles for the king, but even the minutiae of his conduct and appearance in court. Katyayana instructs that the king should enter modestly dressed (*vineeta vesha*), so that litigants are not overwhelmed or intimidated by royal splendour. He was to wear light-coloured garments with minimal adornment and to free himself from attachment or prejudice before adjudicating. According to the jurist Narada, the king, after taking the oath of the son of Vivasvana, must remain impartial towards all beings. The son of Vivasvana is Yama—the god of death—renowned for his absolute impartiality. To swear by Yama was to commit oneself to absolute neutrality.

The selection of judges in ancient India was equally exacting. Beyond mastery of legal theory, the applicant's character and personal conduct were scrutinised. A judge was expected to be austere, restrained, steadfast, impartial, and unwavering in duty. He must not be driven by anger, greed, or desire. He should be truthful, God-fearing, and known for a life of righteousness. Even his family background was examined, not out of elitism, but to ensure that he could not be blackmailed or coerced because of the misconduct of relatives.

Dishonesty in a judge was considered among the gravest of crimes. The punishment for corruption was severe. Brihaspati declares that a judge who accepts bribes or commits injustice must be banished from the state and stripped of his wealth. A corrupt judge, a false witness, and a murderer were placed in the same category of offenders. Even the chief justice was not exempt. If he met privately with a party before a case was concluded, he was to be punished as a corrupt judge.

The intolerance for corruption was matched by an equally robust commitment to procedural fairness. Consequently, the judicial framework of ancient India was structured around strict mechanisms to ensure impartial and objective legal proceedings. All trials were held in open courts, with members of the general public present as observers. To preserve judicial neutrality, the system ensured that a judge had no acquaintance with the litigants, neither friendship nor enmity. Further, to guarantee objectivity, suits were never to be heard by a single judge, not even by the king alone. This highlights that the ancient lawmakers understood that collective deliberation reduces the possibility of corruption and enhances the likelihood of fairness. Accordingly, the rules prescribed that the king must sit with his counsellors while judging cases, and that jurors should sit in benches of uneven numbers—three, five, or seven. All these measures together created an excellent system for safeguarding judicial integrity.

One of the finest features of the ancient Indian judiciary was the appointment of *sabhasadas*, who acted as assessors in the king's court. They may be compared to the present-day jury, yet there was a crucial difference. While modern juries generally consist of laypersons, the sabhasadas were expected to be well versed in legal literature and to possess unimpeachable integrity. They were required to express their opinions fearlessly, even if that meant disagreeing with the king himself. As in modern practice, the innocence or guilt of the accused was determined by these jurors, while the quantum of punishment remained the prerogative of the king. A striking illustration appears in the climax of the ancient Sanskrit drama *Mrichhakatikam* (The Little Clay Cart), where, after pronouncing Charudatta guilty of killing Vasantasena, the judge declares, 'The decision with regard to Charudatta's innocence or guilt lies with us, and our decision is binding, but the rest lies with the sovereign.' Such was the uncompromising moral framework of ancient Indian jurisprudence, where law was not an instrument of power, but a sacred trust. Authority was restrained by ethics, and justice was guarded by those courageous enough to speak truth, even to a king.

The sophistication of the ancient Indian legal system is further evident in its recognition of regional diversity. It acknowledged that customs and practices varied across different parts of the kingdom. Katyayana observed that the state should formally record the customs prevailing in a particular region and authenticate the document with the sovereign's seal. However, this recognition of custom was not absolute. He further stated that if the sovereign became convinced that a particular custom threatened equity, it was to be annulled through a formal decree. This provision reflects a remarkably evolutionary understanding of law, one that rejected the notion of an inflexible and unchanging legal order. Authorities such as Parashara and Manu expressed this idea succinctly through the principle of *yuga roopanusaratah*, asserting that laws must correspond to the age. The laws of the Krita Yuga differed from those of the Treta Yuga, which in turn differed from those of the Dwapara Yuga and the Kali Yuga. In essence, the law was to be revised in accordance with the changing times.

An equally noteworthy aspect of the legal system was its emphasis on prompt justice. The ancient Indian jurists believed that justice delayed is justice denied, and they took deliberate measures to avoid unnecessary postponements in trials and hearings. Their reasoning was not merely ethical but also practical. Katyayana warned against delaying the examination of witnesses, noting that delay weakens memory and fosters imagination. Therefore, the courts accorded the highest importance to the law of evidence and made earnest efforts to ascertain the truth. At a time when many other civilisations relied upon supernatural devices well into the Middle Ages, the ancient Indian courts confined themselves to oral and documentary evidence and firmly rejected supernatural means of proof.

An additional point to note is that truth and honesty were held in such high regard in ancient India that the judge personally administered the oath in the courtroom, unlike today, when it is often performed by a court attendant. While administering the oath, the judge was required to address the witness with an impactful exhortation on the sublime virtue of truthfulness and the fearful karmic consequences of falsehood and perjury. The ancient Greek traveller Megasthenes, as well as the Chinese pilgrims Fa Hien and Huan Tsiang, unequivocally record in their memoirs that the people of ancient India held truth in the highest esteem and practised it in their worldly relations.

Thus, the ingenious ethicists of ancient India aligned the laws and regulations of the state with a higher moral order of dharma, awakening within the people a deep-rooted sense of cosmic responsibility. By this approach, they transformed each individual into a custodian of righteousness. And when one begins to see oneself as spiritually accountable, one naturally strives to honour that calling, becoming a lifelong guardian of ethical living.

Virtue as Duty: How Ancient Principles Guide Modern Ethics

The concepts of rta and dharma represent the uniquely Indian endeavour to ingrain in every individual the conviction that upholding virtues and values is a personal obligation towards oneself and society, not merely the responsibility of the state. The belief that earthly law reflects a grand cosmic order instils magnanimity and seriousness in the pursuit of truth and justice.

In today's landscape, where law is often manipulated by the powerful, the knowledge that there once existed a culture in which even the king stood subject to justice offers reassurance to ordinary people. It reminds us that ethical principles can guide society more effectively than coercion alone and that the moral compass of individuals can uphold fairness even when institutional structures falter. It also highlights the interdependence between personal integrity and collective well-being, suggesting that the smallest ethical choice can ripple outward with far-reaching consequences.

Moreover, the simple awareness that one's actions have the power to affect many lives is sufficient to make us pause and measure our thoughts before turning them into deeds. In this way, even an inward embrace of rta and dharma can bring about a meaningful change in the world, quietly shaping communities, nurturing trust, and fostering a sense of shared responsibility that transcends generations.

Takeaways from the Ancient Past

- Conceiving the sublime concept of dharma as a means of instilling a sense of duty and ethical conduct leads to a good life through conscious choice rather than mere rule-driven imposition.
- Acknowledging that the law stands even above the monarch, and that all beings—including kings and gods—are bound by dharma, helps understand that justice and duty are universal obligations transcending power or position.
- Reciting the hymn 'Loka samasta sukhino bhavantu' to aspire for universal well-being cultivates mindfulness, encourages refraining from harming others, and actively contributes to the happiness of all.

Chapter 9

SOCIETY AND LIFE STAGES

'All creatures are equal in suffering and death.'
—Mahabharata

Varna: Structuring Society with Purpose

The ancient Indians understood that the subtleties of dharma, including law and order, could be implemented only within a well-organised society. The very fact that such principles were sustained for centuries points to the highly evolved social planning of this remarkable civilisation. We will now explore how ancient Indian society functioned with coherence and stability despite its unparalleled complexity and diversity.

Archaeological evidence indicates the presence of organised social life in the Indian subcontinent along the western margins of the Indus river alluvium as early as nine thousand years ago. This eventually evolved into the Indus Valley Civilisation in the third millennium BCE. Over time, the social framework in ancient India was meticulously systematised, demarcating society into four sectors known as *varnas*. The Sanskrit word 'varna' means colour, and it also denotes quality or character. Accordingly, society was classified into brahmins, kshatriyas, vaishyas, and shudras.

In later centuries, this classification came to be identified with the hereditary caste or *jati* system. However, strong textual evidence suggests that in earlier times the division was based primarily on personality, aptitude, and character traits rather than birth. The Bhagavad Gita, revered as the divine utterance of Krishna, declares, 'The four-fold order was created by me according to the divisions of quality and active function.' It further states, 'The works of brahmanas, kshatriyas, vaishyas, and shudras are divided according to the gunas (qualities) born of their own individual nature.' These verses clearly emphasise disposition and action over heredity.

Understanding these principles of disposition and duty allows us to see how early society allocated roles thoughtfully. In practice, the brahmins were priests and scholars inclined towards learning and spirituality; the kshatriyas were warriors and rulers, devoted to martial training, governance, and administration; the vaishyas were merchants, artisans, and entrepreneurs whose aptitude lay in trade, finance, and skilled craftsmanship; and the shudras contributed through physical labour in temples, palaces, farms, and other essential spheres of activity.

Historical records further reinforce the non-hereditary character of the early varna system. Dr D. R. Bhandarkar notes that various foreign tribes entering India were assimilated into different varnas according to their abilities and social roles. Such integration would not have been possible if varna had been rigidly determined by birth. The great epic Mahabharata emphatically states that neither birth, nor rites, nor learning, nor lineage confers the dignity of a brahmin; conduct alone is the true criterion.

Although the classes were clearly distinguished by their primary duties, social mobility was not unattainable. Individual merit and self-transformation could enable a person to rise in stature. Krishna, regarded as the most celebrated personality of his age, was born among the vaishyas and raised in a cowherd household, yet through his intellect and charisma became revered across Bharat. Vyasa, the compiler of the Vedas and author of the Mahabharata, was born to Satyavati, a fisherwoman who later became queen after marrying King Shantanu. Chandragupta Maurya, born to parents of humble origin, rose to establish one of the largest empires in ancient India. Such examples illustrate that while the varna system structured society, it did not make advancement impossible for those of ability and determination.

Thus, both epic literature and historical accounts portray an early varna system that was fluid in spirit and meritocratic in principle, designed not merely to divide society but to organise it harmoniously according to aptitude and duty.

Stages of Life: From Brahmacharya to Sannyasa

An important aspect that governed social life in ancient India was the concept of *ashrama*, according to which human life was divided into four stages. The term ashrama means 'stage' or 'phase.' According to this theory, every individual was expected to pass through four successive stages: brahmacharya (student life), *grihastha* (householder life), *vanaprastha* (retired life), and *sannyasa* (renounced life). These stages were designed to help a person fulfil the four goals of human existence, known as the *purusharthas*: dharma (righteousness), *artha* (wealth and prosperity), *kama* (desires and emotions), and *moksha* (freedom or self-realisation). At the same time, ancient texts also allowed flexibility, suggesting that one could choose to remain in any one of the four ashramas permanently. For instance, a person could remain a *brahmachari* throughout life in the uninterrupted pursuit of knowledge.

As mentioned, brahmacharya represented the stage of student life, traditionally extending up to the age of twenty-five. A brahmachari devoted himself entirely to education and discipline. The student lived in the teacher's hermitage, known in Sanskrit as a gurukulam, where he not only acquired knowledge but also assisted the guru in daily chores. This phase was meant to cultivate both intellectual growth and the spirit of service. Students engaged in cooking, cleaning, and maintaining the hermitage, thereby learning the dignity of labour alongside scholarship. In addition to this, celibacy was observed as a means of practising self-control and discipline. Living away from home also allowed young students to interact with peers from diverse sections of society, learning independence as well as cooperation. In essence, brahmacharya prepared an individual to enter the next stage of life with maturity, responsibility, and social awareness.

Grihastha was the stage of married life and active social participation. It was during this period that one pursued a profession, married, managed a household, raised children, and contributed to society in a dharmic manner. By social ethos, grihastha was considered the most vital of the four stages, for it sustained the entire social structure. It was the phase of intense physical, emotional, occupational, and material engagement. Kautilya describes the duties of a householder as earning a livelihood through one's profession, marrying suitably, maintaining conjugal fidelity, making offerings to gods, ancestors, guests, and dependents, and partaking of what remains. Traditionally extending from twenty-five to fifty years of age, this stage not only encouraged righteous living but also enabled the accumulation of resources necessary for the later phases of life.

Vanaprastha, generally beginning around the age of fifty and continuing until seventy-five, marked the transition into retirement. At this point, the householder gradually handed over responsibilities to the next generation and assumed the role of guide and mentor. The emphasis slowly shifted from artha and kama towards moksha. Life, in this phase, became simpler and more restrained, with reduced indulgence in comforts and a greater focus on essential needs. Through such gradual detachment, the individual prepared inwardly to withdraw from active social life and enter the final stage with serenity.

Sannyasa, traditionally commencing after seventy-five years of age, was the stage of complete renunciation. It involved relinquishing material attachments and emotional bonds in order to dedicate oneself fully to spiritual pursuit. The Mahabharata provides a powerful illustration of this ideal. After the Kurukshetra war, when the Pandavas established their rule, they wished to offer their mother Kunti the comforts of royal life. Yet Kunti, along with other elders of the royal family, chose to retire to the forest. There, they gradually reduced their sustenance and devoted themselves to austerity until they peacefully relinquished their bodies. Such acts were not isolated incidents but reflections of a deeply internalised social philosophy.

Such a holistic approach to life reveals a civilisation that consciously prepared its people for every stage of life. Individuals were trained to move from one phase to another with readiness and dignity, almost as though each transition were a promotion in the journey of the soul. From discipline, study, and self-cultivation during brahmacharya, to active engagement with society and worldly responsibilities during grihastha, to reflection, detachment, and moderation during vanaprastha, ultimately culminating in the pursuit of moksha during sannyasa, the stages of life in ancient India were designed as a continuous journey of growth, responsibility, and spiritual evolution. And in an era when life is often rushed, and transitions between stages are neglected or overlooked, this philosophy offers a profound reminder and a guide to preparing consciously and gracefully for each stage of life.

Redefining Relationships: Divorce, Remarriage, and Social Flexibility

For the ancient Indians, marriage was regarded as the most significant of all the *samskaras*, the rites of passage described in the Dharmashastra texts. *Vivaha*, which literally means the wedding ceremony, attained the full status of marriage when three conditions were fulfilled: the union of husband and wife, the act directed towards procreation, and the establishment of a *kutumba* or family. It marked the sacred transition when the brahmachari and brahmacharini entered the next phase of life together as grihasthas.

In addition, ancient Indian thinkers identified eight distinct forms of marriage. Although all were recognised in theory, they varied greatly in their moral standing and social approval. The Atharva Veda mentions the following types:

1. **Brahma Vivaha**

   Brahma vivaha was considered the most esteemed form of marriage. After completing his education and brahmacharya, a young man was deemed ready for marriage. His parents sought a suitable bride from a respected family, and the girl's father ensured that the prospective groom was learned and worthy. The daughter was given in *kanyadana* without any commercial transaction. This form was held in the highest regard.

2. **Daiva Vivaha**

   Practised particularly among brahmins, this form involved giving a daughter in marriage to a priest who officiated at a sacrificial ritual, often in lieu of a customary fee. Because of this element of exchange, it was considered less auspicious than brahma vivaha.

3. **Arsha Vivaha**

   In this form, the bride was wedded after the groom presented a symbolic gift, typically a cow and a bull. The exchange was modest, yet texts such as those attributed to Manu criticised even this token acceptance, viewing it as a form of sale.

4. **Prajapatya Vivaha**

   Here, the father gave his daughter in marriage with a blessing that the couple might together fulfil their religious duties. In this case, the bride's father actively sought a groom. Though respectable, it was ranked below brahma vivaha in prestige.

5. **Gandharva Vivaha**

   A union based solely on mutual consent, without parental approval or elaborate rituals. In contemporary terms, this resembles a love marriage. The celebrated union of Shakuntala and Dushyanta is often cited as an example.

6. **Asura Vivaha**

   In this arrangement, the bride's family accepted substantial wealth from the groom, often compelling the girl into marriage despite inequality or incompatibility. This form was disapproved because of its overt commercial nature.

7. **Rakshasa Vivaha**

   A marriage effected through abduction and force, often accompanied by violence against the bride's family. The *Dharmashastras* unequivocally condemned this form.

8. **Paishacha Vivaha**

   The most reprehensible of all, *paishacha vivaha* referred to the violation of a woman who was asleep, intoxicated, or otherwise incapacitated. This was regarded as a grave crime and was not accepted as a legitimate marriage.

Thus, while ancient India recognised a spectrum of marital forms, it clearly differentiated between the noble and the ignoble, the ethical and the condemnable.

Besides this, *swayamvara* was a special form of marriage in which a maiden chose her husband from a distinguished assembly of suitors. This practice was most common among royalty and highly influential families. Tradition held that when a princess reached marriageable age and expressed her readiness, the king would dispatch messengers to neighbouring kingdoms announcing the event. On the appointed day, royal suitors gathered in court, and the maiden selected the man of her choice by placing a garland around his neck. The marriage of Damayanti and King Nala is a celebrated example of swayamvara.

Another form involved the declaration of a daughter as *veerashulka*. In this case, the father set forth a formidable challenge, and the suitor who successfully accomplished it, thereby proving his valour and skill, won the bride's hand. In the Ramayana, Rama marries Sita after fulfilling such a challenge, and in the Mahabharata, Arjuna wins Draupadi in a similar manner.

Building on this, the ancient texts often recommended marriage within one's social class. However, inter-class unions were not unheard of, reflecting a flexibility in social practice that sometimes transcended prescriptive norms. For example, Chandragupta Maurya, the founder and first emperor of the Maurya empire, is is said to have entered into a matrimonial alliance with Helena, the daughter of Seleucus. Similarly, the brahmin scholar Vararuchi married a woman of lower social standing on account of her intellect, and their children pursued diverse vocations based on their individual talents. These instances illustrate that marriage in ancient India could accommodate personal choice, merit, and circumstance alongside social conventions.

In general, unions within the same class were preferred, as shared occupation, lifestyle, and social compatibility facilitated stable households. Yet the occurrence of inter-class marriages, among both elites and commoners, shows that social boundaries were not rigidly enforced.

A more universally enforced principle was the prohibition of *sapinda* unions, which forbade marriage between individuals of the same *gotra* (lineage), thereby avoiding close blood relations. The *Agnipurana* explicitly advises against choosing a bride from the same gotra or the line of the same sage and recommends maintaining several generations' distance on both paternal and maternal sides. This practice, aimed at preventing physical or mental abnormalities in offspring, demonstrates a remarkable awareness of the biological consequences of close kinship, long before the formal articulation of genetics.

With regard to conjugal forms, monogamy was the most prevalent and socially approved arrangement in ancient India. It referred to the union of one man and one woman at a given time, and it remained the dominant model from the Vedic age onward. Vatsyayana, the author of the *Kamasutra*, recommends monogamy on the grounds that a man can fully satisfy only one woman physically, emotionally, and spiritually at a time. Rama is revered for observing *ekapatnivrata*—the vow of a single wife—demonstrating absolute fidelity to Sita and refraining from relations with any other woman.

At the same time, polygyny, in which a man had more than one wife, and occasionally polyandry, in which a woman had more than one husband, were also present. Though monogamy was ideal and encouraged, multiple marriages were permitted in certain contexts. In the Mahabharata, each of the Pandava brothers had more than one wife, and all five shared Draupadi as their chief consort.

These examples reveal that ancient India accommodated a wide spectrum of conjugal relationships. At one end stood conventionally arranged marriages, and at the other, unions formed purely by mutual consent, resembling what we might today call cohabitation. Thus, from traditional monogamy to more complex marital arrangements, society displayed a remarkable blend of rootedness in age-old values and openness towards diverse practices.

Additionally, while the dharma schools regarded marriage as a lifelong sacrament, the Artha traditions often treated it as a contractual arrangement entered into by the couple or their guardians. This distinction suggests that the possibility of separation or divorce was not entirely alien to ancient thought. Yajnavalkya states that a woman who undergoes the marriage sacrament a second time is called a *punarbhu*, whether she is a virgin or not. However, a woman who abandoned her husband out of passion for another was termed a *svairini* (denoting unchaste behaviour). Yajnavalkya further observes that in the absence of guardians, a girl may herself choose her bridegroom. Therefore, remarriage, separation under certain conditions, and a woman's right to choose her husband were recognised, even as adultery was censured.

It may also surprise many to learn that widow remarriage was encouraged in Vedic times. In the *Mrityu Suktam* of the Rigveda, the widow is urged to rise from beside her deceased husband and return to the world of the living, with the blessing to seek a new life. Such verses indicate that widow remarriage was neither taboo nor condemned in the earliest layers of tradition.

Taken together, these practices portray a society that normalised divorce, remarriage, and widow remarriage thousands of years ago. It was a society at once structured and flexible, one that offered a clear social framework while still allowing individuals the freedom to shape their personal lives. And within that balance of order and liberty lay its enduring strength.

Navigating Life: A Great Indian Manual for Social Well-Being

Life itself is an abstract journey that arrives without a manual for operation. Yet the ancient seers of India crafted a framework that functioned very much like one, guiding individuals through each phase with clarity and purpose, and thereby reducing confusion and indecision. However, the confronting fact is that in today's world, issues such as midlife crises, difficulty in accepting the decline that comes with old age, the challenge of transferring authority and responsibility, and the loneliness that arises when loved ones move away have become some of the most difficult realities of human existence.

Ancient Indian society offers a roadmap for life, providing holistic guidance on navigating its many stages without prescribing a rigid path. It recognised that life unfolds across multiple dimensions and sought to teach individuals how to engage fully with each phase while preparing gradually for the next. By understanding and embracing the different stages of life, one could maximise personal growth and, over time, ease one's attachment to material pursuits, moving naturally towards introspection and spiritual refinement.

This system, devised thousands of years ago, also reshaped the way one perceives ageing. Rather than seeing it as a loss, dependency on children, or a source of anxiety over wealth and status, individuals were encouraged to cultivate detachment, wisdom, and inner balance. Such a perspective not only nurtured emotional equanimity but also supported better physical and mental health, allowing people to face life's ups and downs with grace. In this way, conscious preparation for each stage of life became essential, forming a lifelong practice of aligning action, reflection, and spiritual growth to live fully at every phase.

Takeaways from the Ancient Past

- Understanding the interest, aptitude, and attitude of every youth and encouraging them to pursue a path suited to their innate capacities ensures that each individual can practise their passion rather than be confined to a rigid mould.
- Dividing human life into four distinct stages while maintaining flexibility to remain in or bypass a stage provides structure without limiting personal freedom, guiding individuals towards growth while respecting their unique paths and capacities.
- Viewing marriage as the coming together of two families and cultural worlds, and attending carefully to social, cultural, economic, and value-based compatibility, allows love and relationships to grow organically over time.

Chapter 10

LOVE AND DESIRE

'Desire can be satisfied only by love, not by force.'
—Kamasutra

Kama: Love Life in Ancient India

As covered in the previous chapter, among the four stages of the ashrama system, the second stage, grihastha (the life of the householder), was given special importance in ancient India. At the heart of this stage lay love: romantic, conjugal, and amorous. The ancient Indians understood that it is the love one shares with a life partner that sustains and enriches the grihastha phase to its fullest potential. Moreover, how could a culture that envisioned universal love overlook one of its most powerful manifestations—carnal love? It is perhaps for this reason that one could write volumes on how deeply the ancients researched, reflected upon, and documented the many dimensions of love.

The idea of love and erotica appears in India as early as prehistoric times. Cave paintings dating back nearly 22,000 years, such as those found in Bhimbetka, depict intimate human forms and unusual postures, suggesting that desire and union were not hidden aspects of life but part of its natural expression. Another cave painting in Kathotia portrays an instance of auto-eroticism. These visual testimonies reveal that ancient Indians neither denied nor suppressed desire; they observed and acknowledged it as an intrinsic force of existence.

Indeed, they believed that love itself was born at the dawn of creation. The god of love was called Kama—a word that signifies passion, desire, affection, lust, and pleasure. The Rigveda describes Kama as *manaso retah* (virility of the mind), indicating that desire originates not merely in the body but in consciousness itself. The Atharva Veda poetically explains that Kama's arrow has wings of mental agony and a shaft fashioned from *sankalpa*, the will or intention for pleasure. Thus, desire was understood as a powerful interplay between mind and body.

In later Puranic literature, Kama is portrayed as exquisitely handsome, wielding a bow of sugarcane strung with honeybees. His banner bears the emblem of the *makara* (the crocodile), symbolising potent vitality, and his quiver contains five arrows tipped with flowers, each representing a progressive stage of desire as shown below:

1. **Aravindam (White Lotus)**

   Aimed at the heart, it induces *harsham*, that is, initial excitement and joy.

2. **Ashokam (Red Saraca Flower)**

   Directed at the lips, it produces *rochanam*, that is, temptation and expressive delight.

3. **Chyutam (Mango Blossom)**

   Aimed at the mind, it causes *sammohanam*, that is, infatuation and enchantment.

4. **Navamalika (Jasmine)**

   Directed at the eyes, it leads to *soshanam*, that is, lovesickness and longing.

5. **Neelotpalam (Blue Lotus)**

   Striking any part of the body, it results in *maranam*, that is, total absorption in love, even to the point of self-forgetfulness.

Such symbolism demonstrates how minutely the ancient seers observed the psychological and emotional phases through which a person passes in love.

The earliest recorded love story also appears in Vedic literature. It narrates the tale of Pururava, a mortal king, and Urvashi, a celestial nymph of extraordinary beauty. At the height of their union, Urvashi leaves him, asserting her independence and her inability to remain bound to a mortal. She promises only the possibility of reunion in heaven after his death. Thus, the world's first documented love story bears the mark of tragedy—a reminder that love, in its intensity, often carries both ecstasy and pain.

Equally intriguing is a brief Vedic dialogue between Yama and his twin sister Yami. Yami, overcome with desire, urges union for the continuation of the human race. Yama, however, refuses on moral grounds, upholding restraint over impulse. This episode reflects that ancient Indian thought did not shy away from exploring even uncomfortable themes; rather, it examined them within a moral and philosophical framework.

Moreover, love and erotica were not confined to art and myth. The Vedic people considered the art of intimacy a refined discipline. One evocative metaphor describes the woman as a sacred fire, her procreative organ as the altar, and union as the spark of ritual fulfilment. Ignorance in the art of lovemaking was seen as undesirable, particularly when the aim was to beget healthy progeny. Detailed standards and guidelines were thus articulated regarding conjugal harmony.

It is therefore unsurprising that ancient India produced the world's first systematic treatise on love and intimacy: the *Kamasutra*, compiled by Vatsyayana. In his work, Vatsyayana acknowledges earlier scholars of *Kamashastra*. He attributes the earliest exposition of the three aims of human life—dharma, artha, and kama—to Prajapati. The section on kama was later condensed by Shvetaketu, then further abridged by Babhravya into one hundred and fifty chapters, and finally organised into seven thematic divisions:

1. *Sadharana* (General principles)
2. *Samprayogika* (Union and intimacy)
3. *Kanyasamprayuktaka* (Courtship)
4. *Bharyadhikarika* (Conjugal life)
5. *Paradarika* (Relations involving others' spouses)
6. *Veshika* (Courtesans)
7. *Aupamishadika* (Aphrodisiacs and allied arts)

Around two millennia ago, Vatsyayana distilled this accumulated wisdom into the *Kamasutra* as we know it today. And far from being merely a manual of physical techniques, it stands as a sophisticated exploration of love as an art, a science, and a vital dimension of human fulfilment within the grihastha stage of life. In the next section, we will delve deeper into how ancient Indian thought understood desire, relationships, and the cultivation of intimacy as integral to a balanced and meaningful life.

Kamasutra: Vatsyayana's Comprehensive Guide to Love

Kamasutra is the oldest surviving—and perhaps the only holistic, systematic, and encyclopaedic—treatise on the art and science of lovemaking to this day. Vatsyayana composed this remarkable work after undertaking research that was rigorous and far-reaching by any standard. In the concluding chapter, he explains that he wrote the book after meticulously collecting and studying the works of earlier subject experts, observing men and women in pleasure houses, and yet remaining celibate himself so that he could approach every aspect of lovemaking with objectivity. This underscores the fact that the *Kamasutra* is far more than a manual of sexual positions, as it is often misunderstood today. It is a prolific guide to the art of living well: the nature of love, the nuances of social engagement, the methods of finding a suitable partner, the subtleties of courtship and flirtation, the cultivation of an active conjugal life, and the dynamics of power within marriage. It also discusses the conditions under which adultery may occur, elaborate forms of foreplay, diverse sexual postures, and other dimensions of leading a desirous yet socially embedded life.

Extending beyond general advice on love, the *Kamasutra* provides detailed guidance on matching partners for optimal compatibility. The text classifies men and women into categories based on personality, body type, the size and shape of their genital organs, and their level of desire. On the basis of these characteristics, Vatsyayana prescribes compatible unions and explains why such pairings would heighten pleasure and contribute to a long-lasting and harmonious married life.

Kamasutra also specifies the appropriate age for receiving knowledge of the sexual act, the arts that refine one's rapport with a partner, and the etiquette for approaching a potential companion. Vatsyayana emphasises that the key to a successful conjugal relationship lies in the attitude of 'giving pleasure' rather than 'seeking pleasure for oneself.' When both partners adopt this disposition, intimacy becomes a creative celebration.

Additionally, an entire section is devoted to personal hygiene before and after sexual union, as well as to the preparation and decoration of the space in which the couple engages in lovemaking. The text describes various forms of *alingana* (embraces) in standing, sitting, reclining, and other positions. It details twenty-six types of *chumbana* (kisses), each serving a specific purpose and involving distinct movements of the lips, mouth, or tongue at different stages of intimacy.

To deepen mutual arousal, Vatsyayana also discusses the controlled introduction of mild pain, including *nakhachhedya* (fingernail marks), *dantachhedya* (bite marks), and various forms of gentle striking or tapping intended to stimulate particular nerves.

Drawing inspiration from the animal world, the ancient Indians observed diverse mating behaviours and adapted certain elements to refine human lovemaking. At the same time, Vatsyayana clearly cautions men against attempting such practices during the early days of marriage. The text insists on proceeding at the woman's pace, building her confidence gradually, and ensuring her consent and comfort at every stage.

Kamasutra also outlines techniques of oral intimacy and describes a wide range of postures during sexual union, from the simple and conventional to the complex and unconventional. While encouraging exploration and experimentation, it carefully notes contraindications for specific postures, including stages of pregnancy, particular body types, illness, or fever.

Significantly, the text addresses homosexual unions, both male-male and female-female, and provides guidance for transgender individuals in matters of intimacy. It also mentions the use of artificial devices to enhance sexual experience and discusses techniques of auto-eroticism, indicating the types of individuals and circumstances for which such methods may be appropriate.

The book further explores situations in which the woman assumes the traditionally masculine role in lovemaking and reflects on the role of playful quarrels in rekindling affection. It concludes by discussing the duties of husbands and wives, the characteristics expected of men and women in married life, the value of fidelity, the circumstances under which extramarital relationships may arise, and the questions of bereavement and remarriage.

Ultimately, *Kamasutra* declares that its purpose is to sustain and elevate excitement within marriage so that mutual interest does not diminish over time. It presents itself as a comprehensive guide to nurturing enduring love, vitality, and fidelity within the marital union.

Ganika: The Revered Courtesan Tradition

In ancient India, there existed a unique category of women known as the *ganikas*. While the word 'ganika' may be loosely translated as courtesan or public woman, in the Indian context, she represented something far more refined and elevated. A ganika was a *nagaravadhu*—the bride of the city—renowned not only for her beauty but also for her education and accomplishments. She was trained in the sixty-four arts, which included dance, music, history, politics, oration, poetry, logic, and the art of seduction, among many others. And unlike women who were groomed primarily for marriage, a ganika chose to remain single and enjoyed the freedom to select her own companions. Distinguished and wealthy men sought her company not merely for physical pleasure, but for intellectual engagement, aesthetic delight, and sophisticated conversation. The ganika was also honoured by the king and admired by discerning men who could recognise excellence. In fact, ganikas enjoyed such respect that they could be invited to participate in assemblies of men to deliberate on matters of state. In many ways, she became the observer of all observers and a model of refinement and cultural accomplishment.

Arguably, the most celebrated ganika of ancient India was Amrapali, the famed courtesan of Vaishali, the capital of the Licchavi republic. The wealth and influence she commanded rivalled that of the most illustrious men of her time. Her retinue was vast, her palace opulent, and her carriages as magnificent as those of the ruling elite, against whom she drove axle to axle, wheel to wheel, and yoke to yoke. Amrapali came to embody an institution integral to the civic and cultural life of the city. Such was her stature that Bimbisara, the king of Magadha, is said to have instituted the tradition of the ganika in his own capital, Rajagriha, inspired by her example.

Notably, Vatsyayana in *Kamasutra* and Bharata in *Natyashastra* describe in detail the qualities that distinguished an ideal ganika from an ordinary courtesan, including her intelligence, learning, demeanour, and social grace. Wealthy and independent, she possessed the means to sponsor public works such as hospitals, water tanks, gardens, bridges, and temples. On the whole, the ganika represented not merely aesthetic refinement but also a powerful model of female agency and social participation.

Pleasure and Partnership: A Comprehensive Approach to Intimacy

As noted earlier, unlike many other ancient cultures, the Indians approached love and intimacy with a distinctive openness, imagination, and creativity. They believed that the longevity of marriage depended significantly on physical harmony and mutual satisfaction. To this end, they created a structured manual capable of guiding even inexperienced couples through the complexities of conjugal intimacy, enabling them gradually to understand and fulfil one another's needs.

In contrast, many modern manuals claiming inspiration from the *Kamasutra*, as well as segments of the erotica industry, often promote unrealistic standards that can foster dissatisfaction and imbalance between partners. This makes it all the more important to revisit the original work and appreciate its significance. *Kamasutra* offers a thoughtful reference point, especially at a time when many relationships struggle due to a lack of understanding of a partner's body, temperament, and emotional world. It moves beyond rigid binaries to recognise a spectrum of gender and sexual possibilities and extends far beyond the physical act to address personal hygiene, emotional attitude, and the creation of a harmonious and appropriate ambience.

Kamasutra thus stands not merely as a treatise on erotic technique, but as a comprehensive guide to cultivating a creative, respectful, and enduring love life that harmonises desire with dignity, pleasure with partnership, and intimacy with mutual growth. It encourages couples to set aside ego during intimacy and to approach one another as equals engaged in a shared exploration of pleasure and happiness.

Takeaways from the Ancient Past

- Regarding love and lovemaking as arts to be studied and practised with seriousness, and composing systematic guidance for couples, cultivates and sustains conjugal harmony.
- Encouraging couples to relate as playful companions and set aside inhibitions within their private union fosters honest, creative communication and prevents many difficulties in relationships today.
- Presenting pleasure as a shared experience, equally desired by both partners, and emphasising the responsibility of giving pleasure, elevates intimacy beyond personal gratification and nurtures mutual fulfilment.
- Honouring women who pursue their chosen paths with sincerity and dedication recognises talent, integrity, and ambition regardless of gender, inspiring women to stand confidently and achieve influence alongside men.

Chapter 11

ARCHITECTURE AND RITUAL

'The one who knows the Supreme Being as residing in the cave of the heart, in the highest shrine, knows all.'
—Mundaka Upanishad

Sacred Architecture and Living Ritual: The Temple as Cosmos in Stone

In ancient India, self-reflection and introspection were integral to daily life. This emphasis on inner awareness influenced both private and communal spaces. Households often included simple areas for quiet contemplation, while communities built *mandira* (temples) as centres for collective worship and shared reflection.

What stands out is that temples were conceived as a re-creation of the primordial universe—the very womb of creation—imbued with the positive energy of the divine. This vision shaped not only their architecture but also their rituals, reflecting the profound interconnectedness between the individual and the cosmos. Principles of design, proportion, orientation, and measurement were meticulously applied to optimise the flow of positive energy both within the structure and within those who entered it. In terms of complexity, precision, durability, aesthetic refinement, ecological sensitivity, and symbolic depth, these temples achieved a level of mastery unparalleled in the ancient world. Entering a temple was therefore far more than a ritual act; it was a philosophical experience, inviting devotees to contemplate the microcosm within the macrocosm and to recognise that the same universal energy sustaining the cosmos also resides within themselves.

Archaeological evidence suggests that sacred spaces of worship existed in ancient India as early as the Bronze Age, roughly 5,500 years ago. The master architects of the time codified their knowledge in two principal groups of texts: the *Vastushastras*, which dealt with architecture and spatial harmony, and the *Shilpashastras*, which focused on sculpture, iconography, and painting. Their foundations can be traced to the Sthapatya Veda, which is regarded as a branch of the Atharva Veda and revered as the sacred science of architecture and construction.

In keeping with these sacred principles, temple sites were also chosen with meticulous attention to natural beauty and ecological balance. Authoritative texts describe the ideal site for a temple as one situated near pristine waters and flourishing gardens, where lotus and wildflowers bloom, where swans, ducks, parrots, cuckoos, and other birds are heard, and where animals rest without fear, for such places were believed to be the playgrounds of the gods. River confluences were considered especially sacred, though caves, hilltops, and mountain slopes were also favoured locations.

Most temples also included an artificially constructed pond connected to nearby natural water sources through underground channels. Devotees bathed, or at least washed their feet, hands, and face, before entering the sanctum. Priests, too, performed ritual ablutions in these waters before commencing worship.

Together, these practices reveal that ancient Indian sacred architecture was not just about buildings, but about creating harmonious spaces that nurtured the body, mind, and spirit. Every element—from location and layout to water and wildlife—was thoughtfully designed to reflect cosmic order and invite a sense of reverence and tranquillity.

Built to Elevate: Temples as Charging Stations for the Human Spirit

In ancient India, temple construction was a highly collaborative and meticulously organised endeavour, blending artistry, engineering, and spiritual vision. Every structure was conceived as a reflection of cosmic order, where architecture, symbolism, and spiritual philosophy converged to create spaces meant to inspire awe and facilitate spiritual growth.

The construction of temples was undertaken by organised guilds of architects, artisans, and labourers. These guilds functioned much like corporate bodies, establishing standards of work and regulating wages. The enterprise was led by a *sutradhara* (chief architect), supported by construction superintendents. Among the key members were the chief stonemason and the chief image-maker. Women, too, participated in these collaborative efforts. Together, in remarkable coordination, they created monumental structures designed to endure not merely for generations but for millennia.

Furthermore, the design and construction of ancient temples were marked by extraordinary precision, reflecting not only spiritual devotion but also remarkable scientific insight. Far from being mere places of worship, these structures embodied India's advancements in physics, chemistry, biology, astronomy, architecture, and mathematics. Master builders integrated sophisticated innovations into every aspect of their work, ensuring that form, function, and symbolism existed in harmonious balance. Visionary kings, in turn, patronised these monumental creations to honour the divine while also establishing enduring legacies for their dynasties. Yet beyond their architectural grandeur and engineering brilliance, it is their symbolism that makes them truly magnificent. Every temple was envisioned as a spiritual being, a meditating yogi in three dimensions, at once lying supine and seated in *padmasana*.

As for the temple complex, it often included a circumambulatory passage for *parikrama* or *pradakshina*, which may be seen as the body of the yogi. The *dhwaja sthambha*, or flagpole, represents the backbone, and the main shrine forms the head. This innermost shrine, known worldwide as the sanctum sanctorum, is called the *garbhagriha* in Sanskrit. While 'sanctum sanctorum' means 'the holy of holies,' the word 'garbhagriha' literally translates to 'womb chamber.'

The distinction in design between outer opulence and inner austerity is profound. The outer structure of the temple is often elaborately carved with intricate sculptures and ornamentation. In contrast, the inner walls of the garbhagriha are plain stone—an excavated hollow space, entirely dark, stripped of embellishment, an embodied nothingness. This void symbolises the primordial moment of creation, the first stirrings of the universe, the beginning of time itself. The garbhagriha thereby represents the cosmic womb from which all creation emerges, the epicentre of universal creative energy.

Within this womb resides the *murti* or *vigraha* (the idol of the chief deity). The vigraha is crafted by specially chosen artisans who observe strict *vratam* (disciplined vows) throughout the period of its creation. They are housed in specially prepared chambers near the shrine site for the entire duration of the work. The idol may be sculpted from stone, cast in bronze, fashioned in gold or silver, or created from *panchaloha* (a sacred alloy of five auspicious metals). In rare cases, other unique combinations of substances are used, each selected according to meticulous prescriptions laid down in traditional texts.

As the artisan sculpts or moulds the idol, priests assemble reverently around the work in progress and chant potent Vedic mantras for hours, three times a day. Through this sustained invocation, the vibrational power of sacred sound is believed to infuse the idol with positive energy. Modern research may now explore the influence of sound on matter, yet these ancient masters had long understood and harnessed this subtle principle in their consecratory practices.

Upon completion, the idol is ceremonially installed within the garbhagriha through elaborate Vedic rites. It is firmly fixed to the pedestal, whose foundation extends deep into the earth, using a specially prepared compound of eight adhesive substances known as *ashtabandham*. Therefore, within the silent, windowless darkness of the womb chamber, the deity—the universal spirit—is symbolically and ritually born.

Devotees would then visit the temple to see the deity within the garbhagriha. This act of sacred seeing is called *darsanam*, a word that signifies not merely sight, but vision infused with knowledge. The same term was also used by ancient scholars to denote philosophy, implying the seeing of truth. In both contexts, the act is not limited to physical perception but extends to inner experience and understanding.

Standing before the garbhagriha, where ultimate reality is symbolically made manifest, the devotee would gaze upon the deity and reflect deeply. This became a moment of contemplation, an inward turning of awareness. This practice resonates with the Upanishadic declaration, 'Ayam Atma Brahma (This self is Brahman).' Each darsanam thus serves as an affirmation that the universal energy of the divine resides within oneself. And it is this sublime and optimistic vision that enables the seeker to shed negativity and be replenished with serene positivity. In fact, the primary aim of the ancient builders and seers who designed both the temple architecture and the ritual of darsanam was to deliberately inspire this inner transformation.

It is worth noting that while such contemplation could take place anywhere, garbhagriha spaces provided an unmatched environment for deep immersion. Its darkness, silence, and symbolic depth eliminated external distractions and heightened internal awareness. In that sacred space, the deity—resplendent in sound, fragrance, light, and form served as the focal point of meditation, guiding the devotee inward on a journey toward clarity, strength, and the refinement of character.

In this way, darsanam became more than simply seeing the deity. It evolved into a process of seeing oneself honestly, deeply, and aspirationally. This practice went beyond the boundaries of religion and ritual, becoming a disciplined exercise in self-envisioning.

Another point worth noting is that, from the smallest shrine in a remote village to the grand temples or *mahakshetras*, every temple functioned as a guardian presence and a moral anchor for the people of that land. It was not merely a place of worship, but a living centre of cultural and spiritual identity. Moreover, the deity chosen for each temple was never arbitrary; it carried deep significance connected to the region's history, geography, and the collective aspirations of its people.

When it came to worshipping the deity, the process began at Brahma Muhurtam, the sacred hour before dawn. The priest commenced the rituals with the ceremonial bathing of the deity in well water, a rite known as *nirmalyam*, symbolising purification and renewal. The deity was then adorned with fresh garments, jewellery, and newly plucked flowers. Lamps were lit within the garbhagriha using ghee or sesame oil with cotton wicks, filling the sanctum with warmth and radiance. Frankincense and camphor were burned, infusing the space with a sacred fragrance. Throughout these rites, the priest chanted Vedic mantras specific to the presiding deity, invoking and sustaining the divine presence through sound. Large brass bells resounded across the temple precincts, their rhythm merging with the chants to create a deep vibration felt in the body and mind of every devotee present.

The deity was then symbolically offered specially prepared food. Once offered, it became *nivedyam* or *prasadam*, sanctified nourishment that was later distributed among the devotees. This was followed by the puja proper, with elaborate chanting, floral offerings, ritual ablutions, and fire consecration, while devotees lined up before the garbhagriha for darsanam. During the height of the ritual, the doors of the sanctum remained closed. At the climactic moment, they were opened from within to the resonant peal of temple bells, revealing the deity in spiritual splendour for devotees to behold and inwardly absorb.

The ceremony concluded with the waving of a camphor flame before the deity. The priest then stepped out and sprinkled the devotees with the sanctified water collected from the ablution of the idol. The camphor flame was brought forth for devotees to touch reverentially. Through these gestures, the divine energy invoked within the garbhagriha was symbolically shared with the community. The ritual thus created a sacred bond between the many and the One.

Another important ritual was the *sheeveli*. In addition to the main fixed deity, each garbhagriha housed a smaller portable idol known as the *sheeveli vigraha*. During this ceremony, the miniature deity was carried out either on a palanquin or borne upon the priest's head. Accompanied by attendants, the deity in this portable form circumambulated the temple three times. This act symbolised the deity's benevolent survey of the well-being of all beings and subtle presences within the temple precincts, and by extension, the entire village. After the circumambulation, the deity was returned to the sanctum, and the temple doors were closed for the day.

This sacred cycle, beginning with nirmalyam in the early hours and culminating in sheeveli in the evening, unfolded each day without fail. During annual festivals, the deity emerged in an elaborate procession and circumambulated the entire village or region, symbolically visiting households and blessing the land. In this way, the temple and its deity became exemplars of disciplined living, responsibility, and compassionate guardianship, setting a standard for daily conduct and collective harmony.

We will now turn to three iconic temples of the ancient Indian subcontinent, examining some of their most remarkable features so that the full extent of their technological sophistication and architectural mastery can be truly appreciated.

1. Padmanabha Swamy Temple

Located in present-day Thiruvananthapuram, Kerala, the idol of the chief deity of the Sree Padmanabha Swamy Temple is truly one of a kind. The deity of this millennia-old temple is Lord Vishnu in the *anantasaayi* posture, depicted reclining in cosmic repose upon the thousand-headed serpent Ananta, symbolising his transcendental slumber amidst the eternal rhythm of creation. The idol stretches an astounding eighteen feet in length and is revealed to devotees through three adjacent doors: the head and neck through the first, the torso through the second, and the legs through the third.

At the very core of the idol are placed 12,008 perfectly selected *saligramams*, which are fossilised ammonite stones found in the Gandaki River in Nepal, each revered as an aniconic form of Vishnu. These sacred stones were chosen from among thousands and brought ritualistically from Nepal to the southernmost tip of the Indian subcontinent. Around this powerful nucleus was built an extraordinarily intricate structure using 108 natural substances through the ancient technique known as *Katu Sharkara Yogam*.

Employing natural materials, medicinal herbs, lacs, and carefully sourced sands and soils from different regions, the artisans recreated the human form in remarkable detail, constructing the skeleton, musculature, blood vessels, nerves, and finally the skin. To appreciate the precision and layered complexity of this craftsmanship, let us take a closer look at the various stages involved in the making of the idol.

Mrctha Lepana, or mud layering, begins with the collection of soil from three distinct terrains: dry land, marshland, and desert. Each type is blended with a specific *kashayam*, which is a complex herbal decoction, and allowed to rest for ten days. To this mixture is added pristine river sand and water from the course of the Ganga, along with other prescribed ingredients. The blend is then combined with preparations derived from the Ilippa tree (*Madhuca longifolia*) and rested again.

What then emerges is a medicinally potent mud, which is applied over the skeletal framework of the idol to create musculature and form. Afterwards, a layer of pure silk is wrapped finely around it before the final outer layer—symbolising the skin—is added. This topmost surface is so dark that the idol appears almost pitch black, merging visually with the equally dark interior of the garbhagriha.

The most extraordinary aspect of Katu Sharkara Yogam is its extreme sensitivity to water. No liquid ablutions are performed for the deity, for water could dissolve the structure itself. Even the flowers used for adornment are carefully shaken the previous night to ensure that not a single drop of moisture remains.

Thus, the idol at Padmanabha Swamy represents the pinnacle of human craftsmanship while remaining entirely natural in composition, preserved in astonishing perfection, and seemingly defying the passage of time.

2. Kailasa Temple

The Kailasa Temple, also known as Cave 16, is one of the thirty-four cave temples and monasteries that together form the Ellora Caves in present-day Maharashtra. Commissioned around 1,300 years ago by the Rashtrakuta king Krishna I, it remains the largest monolithic structure ever created by human hands.

Measuring 164 feet in length, 108 feet in width, and rising to a height of 96 feet, the temple was carved entirely out of a single rock using a vertical excavation technique. The work began from the top and progressed downward. Such a method demanded flawless planning, for once the chiselling began, there was no scope for correction. Not a single stone fragment could be replaced, and not a single miscalculation could be undone. Every measurement, every pillar, every sculptural detail had to be envisioned in its entirety before the first strike of the chisel.

This multi-storeyed complex is dedicated to Lord Shiva and symbolically represents Mount Kailasa, his celestial abode. Originally, the entire structure was coated with a thick layer of pure white plaster to create the illusion of snow-clad brilliance, echoing the Himalayan peak it sought to emulate. Even today, faint traces of this plaster remain, whispering of the temple's once resplendent façade.

The temple is carved out of an extremely hard volcanic basalt cliff, a material that is difficult to work with even today. Though archaeologists estimate that such a megastructure should have taken more than a century to complete, it was accomplished in an astonishing eighteen years. Nearly 200,000 tonnes, or 20 crore kilograms, of rock had to be removed from the cliff to bring this monument into being. This means that the ancient builders chiselled away approximately 11,000 tonnes a year, or close to 30,000 kilograms every single day. And this calculation does not even account for the time required to execute the extraordinarily intricate carvings and sculptural details that adorn the entire complex.

Covering an area nearly twice the size of the Parthenon in Athens, Greece, the temple continues to puzzle historians who wonder how such speed and precision were achieved without modern technology. The answer perhaps lies in the astonishing sophistication of planning, geometry, and execution that is visible in every inch of the structure. One is further reminded of its resilience by the account of an invader who reportedly ordered its demolition; a thousand men laboured for three years yet failed to cause any significant damage. This is why the Kailasa Temple stands as one of the proudest testaments to Indian temple-building excellence.

3. Kamakhya Temple

Located in present-day Guwahati, Assam, the Kamakhya Temple is among the most important centres of the goddess tradition and one of the oldest and most revered seats of tantric practice.

Majestically overlooking the Brahmaputra River, the temple's exterior is richly carved, yet as one moves inward, the space gradually becomes more austere, dim, and narrow, until one finally descends into the underground garbhagriha. Within this subterranean chamber resides a most unique deity: an aniconic yoni, a natural cleft in the rock floor that is perpetually filled with water from a spring deep within the earth. In the dim light, devotees do not 'see' the deity in the conventional sense. Instead, they touch the sacred water within the opening, receiving a deeply tactile form of darsanam. This millennia-old shrine venerates fertility and the creative power of the divine feminine, the Mother Earth herself.

Here, the goddess is believed to undergo her annual menstruation for three days, during which the temple remains closed. Tantric practitioners and devotees from across the country gather in anticipation, waiting for the period to conclude and for the sanctum to reopen. This sacred observance is known as *ambubachi*, meaning 'spoken with water,' and it coincides with the monsoon season. During these days, the Brahmaputra is said to swell and even turn reddish, symbolically reflecting the divine menses.

In reverence to this cosmic cycle, the local community refrains from cooking so as not to generate heat and also abstains from farming so as not to wound the earth. Nature herself is believed to be resting. When the three days conclude, the rains follow, signifying renewed fertility and affirming that the goddess is ready to create and the earth is ready to yield. On the fourth day, the temple doors reopen, and the sacred water from the yoni is distributed among devotees, symbolically diffusing the creative energy of the goddess across the land. In this way, ritual, ecology, and feminine divinity converge into a single sacred vision.

Within this broader spiritual framework, the Kamakhya Temple emerges as a profound example of nature worship, celebrating the feminine as the supreme creative force.

In summary, the engineering geniuses of ancient India—through sophisticated construction materials and design, carefully codified mantras that generated potent vibrational energies, and rituals that elevated the human mind from the mundane to the ethereal—conceived temples as reservoirs of positive energy. These sacred spaces functioned as centres where devotees could recharge themselves, not through any mechanical means, but through deep spiritual introspection. In this sense, the ancient temple was nothing less than a charging station for the human spirit.

Takeaways from the Ancient Past

- Visiting temples, which are sacred and serene sanctuaries, helps step away from daily distractions and turn inward, fostering focus on the self and holistic spiritual growth.
- Observing the deity in each temple as a living role model, and reflecting on the care and empathy it extends to all beings, encourages one to cultivate those same qualities in one's own life.
- Experiencing the structure, ambience, and rituals of the temple as a source of positive energy allows one to lay aside fatigue, neutralise negativity, and return to daily life renewed and inwardly strengthened.

Chapter 12

FESTIVALS AND CELEBRATIONS

'By renouncing, enjoy.'

—Isha Upanishad

Utsava: Festivals in Ancient India

From all the themes we have explored so far, it should not appear that ancient Indians were solemn people bound by rigid discipline and unyielding routine. On the contrary, they observed numerous festivals (*utsava*) throughout the year and organised elaborate, vibrant celebrations. To use modern lingo, they certainly knew how to party.

The Sanskrit word 'utsava' is derived from ut, meaning 'to start,' and sava, meaning 'change.' Thus, every new beginning was welcomed as a festival in ancient India. They celebrated changes in nature, shifts in seasons, and significant astronomical events. While many popular festivals from that era continue even today, there were also unique and fascinating celebrations that every lover of nature and culture ought to know.

1. Vasantotsava

Among the most celebrated was the spring festival, Vasantotsava. On the first day of the month of Chaitra, when nature undergoes its charming transformation—creepers adorning themselves with fragrant blossoms, honeybees humming over flowers, woods swaying to playful gusts of wind, and valleys echoing with the melodious songs of the cuckoo and the golden oriole—the poetic transition into spring was marked with festivity. The celebrations often stretched across a day or two. Festive processions were organised in which flags were ceremoniously raised and lowered. Freshly prepared vermilion was tossed into the air at intervals, symbolising the vibrant hues that spring would soon unfold.

As the procession moved through the main streets of the city, people joined in, singing and dancing to rhythmic drumbeats. Several processions from different quarters would converge at the central garden, where the community gathered to welcome the new season together. A popular game involved making balls or bunches of flowers. The chasers would attempt to strike the runners with these floral clusters, while the runners tried to evade them. The king, his royal consorts, ministers, and the entire royal retinue would also participate in the festivities, joining the common folk in celebration and play.

Vasantotsava thus marked an annual transition filled with hope for a resplendent blooming season, hope for abundant fruit, and hope for a generous harvest.

2. Marotsava

Another important celebration was *Marotsava*, the festival of the god of love, Kama—also known as Mara—observed annually on the thirteenth day of the bright fortnight of Chaitra. This festival was celebrated by single men and women who expressed reverence to Mara in the hope of inviting pure love into their lives. Married and unmarried couples also observed it in gratitude for the love they had found.

In this spirit of gratitude and festivity, the celebration unfolded in vivid and joyous expression. People dressed in vibrant colours, especially shades of red, adorned themselves with fragrant garlands and jewellery, and gathered around the temple of Kama to offer worship. Thereafter, they entered the temple pond or a nearby water body and engaged in various water sports and playful games. The evening and night were spent singing, dancing, drinking wine, watching wrestling matches, and enjoying love-themed dramas. It was also the occasion when the brave among them expressed their heartfelt emotions to those they secretly cherished.

3. Makara Sankranti

Another significant festival was Makara Sankranti, an auspicious day determined by the solar cycle. It corresponds to the astronomical transition of the sun from the zodiac of Sagittarius (*Dhanu*) to Capricorn (*Makara*). As this shift also marks the sun's northward journey, the festival is dedicated to the sun god Surya and symbolises renewal and new beginnings. This period of the year has long been considered especially conducive to spiritual practice.

Marking this auspicious juncture, people gathered along riverbanks to bathe in pristine waters and cleanse themselves in preparation for renewed spiritual discipline. For this reason, Snanotsava, the bathing festival, formed an essential part of Sankranti. And beyond spiritual discourse and philosophical dialogue, these gatherings also featured dance and music festivals, kite flying, bonfires, and grand feasts, bringing together devotion, celebration, commerce, and community in a remarkable expression of life's fullness.

Moreover, every twelve years, Makara Sankranti is observed with the Kumbha Mela, a grand pilgrimage dedicated to Surya and to ritual bathing at one of four sacred sites: Prayaga, Haridwar, Nashik, and Ujjain. Ancient Indian astronomers calculated the revolution of Jupiter (*Brihaspati*) as twelve years, and the Kumbha Mela marks the completion of one such revolution, adding cosmic significance to the observance. When Jupiter completes twelve revolutions, once every 144 years, the Mahakumbha Mela takes place at Prayaga, at the sacred confluence of the Ganga, Yamuna, and the mystical Saraswati.

Also, as this season coincides with the mid-winter harvest, large fairs known as *melas* are organised along riverbanks. Merchants, farmers, and artisans display and sell the finest products of their land. An interesting fact is that the Mahabharata refers to the organisation of the Magha Mela, attesting to its great antiquity.

In addition, the Makara Sankranti and the Kumbha Mela reveal the remarkable astronomical awareness of the people of ancient India. In those times, almost every household possessed a text known as the *Panchanga*, a work rooted in astronomy and astrology. More than a book, it functioned as a calendar or diary, detailing the auspicious days of the year and recording the daily positions of planets and constellations. Without announcements or public proclamations, people instinctively knew when Sankranti had arrived, and villagers would gather at the main riverbank of their settlement. Likewise, without any formal summons, every twelve years, people from across the Indian subcontinent journeyed to the designated site of the Kumbha Mela to take the sacred dip. In that moment, nature bore witness to millions of individuals, diverse in language and background, united by a single resolve: self-purification and gratitude to the elemental cleansers, the water and the sun.

4. **Indrotsava**

Indrotsava was another prominent festival observed in ancient India, dedicated to Indra, the Vedic deity associated with rain, thunder, and lightning. As annual rains were vital for agriculture, this festival became a collective effort to ensure abundant rainfall in the coming year. The celebrations began with the erection of a flagpole (*dhwaja sthambha*) and the hoisting of a flag bearing Indra's emblem. People gathered around the flagpole and performed *udakadaana*, the ritual donation of water. Each person offered a small bowl of water to another, and the receiver reverently drank the offering. This act symbolised the indispensable role of water in sustaining life and affirmed that this precious resource belonged to all and was divine in its essence.

The festival then moved from symbolism to action. People formed groups, cleaned ponds and water tanks, tidied gardens, and prepared farmlands for cultivation. After a day of collective labour, they assembled once more to sing rain songs, perform dances themed around the monsoon, and partake in hearty meals. In this way, they prepared both their cities and themselves to welcome the forthcoming rains.

Thus, it becomes evident that by blending ritual, worship, entertainment, and merrymaking, the ancient Indians ingeniously wove nature conservation, industriousness, and social unity into the heart of every celebration. Each festival became a means of revering and protecting Mother Nature, while instilling a sense of ecological responsibility from childhood. And at a deeper level, these celebrations symbolised the graceful acceptance of change in nature, a reminder of the ever-changing rhythm of human life itself.

Joy in Harmony: Festivals as a Celebration of Life and Environment

Why do human communities cherish festivals and celebrations? Because we long to gather, to rejoice, to share moments of collective joy. The ancient Indians understood this intrinsic celebratory impulse and wrapped it beautifully around the profound core of nature conservation. By worshipping natural elements as divine, they cultivated an unwavering sense of duty to revere and protect them. Their celebrations were exuberant and enticing, filled with music, dance, theatre, food, drink, and games, creating irresistible multisensorial experiences while preserving the sanctity of the natural world.

This seamless blending of celebration and conservation reveals a wisdom that feels strikingly contemporary. Today, nations across the world strive to make their festivals greener and more environmentally responsible. Yet thousands of years ago, ancient India had already embraced this ethos. They did not merely make their festivals nature-friendly; they celebrated nature itself. And if such a spirit once shaped an entire civilisation, it can surely find a place in our lives today. What if each of us chose one day every month—one personally meaningful to you—as a day dedicated to celebrating nature in simple, conscious ways? What if you, alone or with your loved ones, observed that day in a consciously nature-friendly manner, without disrupting your routine? It could be as simple as watering a few plants in your neighbourhood, feeding seeds or fruits to birds, placing a handful of grains outside for ants, planting saplings along the roadside, or lying on your terrace at night and conversing with the moon and stars in gratitude for their quiet beauty.

The intention at the heart of such a practice is simple: to consciously restore a forgotten intimacy with the natural world. Such small, deliberate acts can soften our habits of indifference and remind us that we are participants, not spectators, in the web of life. When performed regularly, even once a month, they can gradually reshape our sensibilities, cultivating humility, responsibility, and quiet joy. In rekindling this primaeval friendship with nature, we do not merely protect the environment; we rediscover a deeper harmony within ourselves.

Takeaways from the Ancient Past

- Living in harmony with nature and regarding every shift in the natural world as a reason to rejoice teaches us how to observe and align with the rhythms of nature in daily life.
- Grounding utsavas in the principle of conservation and encouraging the preservation and equitable sharing of natural resources demonstrates how celebrations can honour both joy and responsibility towards the environment.
- Incorporating joyous entertainment and inclusive activities that engage all age groups shows that sustainability becomes most effective when practised collectively and with a sense of shared delight.

Chapter 13

MARTIAL ARTS AND DISCIPLINE

'The greatest enemy is the one within.'

—Mahabharata

Kalari: The Mother of All Martial Arts

The ancient Indians were a people deeply fascinated by nature. Their curiosity extended not only to the nature that surrounded them but also to the nature within. They perceived the human body as the delicate interface between these two—yet essentially one—dimensions of nature. It is therefore no surprise that they explored every possibility to protect the body and to strengthen it to extraordinary levels. In this spirit of physical discipline and self-mastery, ancient India developed one of the earliest martial traditions in the world.

Kalaripayattu, often simply called Kalari, originated on the south-western coast of India, in present-day Kerala, around the third century BCE. Its conceptual precursors can be traced to the Dhanurveda—the ancient treatise on warfare and archery associated with the Yajurveda—compiled around 1100 BCE and attributed to sages such as Bhrigu, Vishvamitra, and Bharadwaja. With such a lineage, Kalari is frequently described as the 'mother of all martial arts' and is believed to have influenced later traditions such as kung fu and karate.

Historical narratives also suggest that the legacy of Indian martial knowledge travelled far beyond the subcontinent. Among the most intriguing accounts is that of a prince-turned-monk named Bodhidharma of the Pallava dynasty who journeyed to China around the fifth century CE. Chinese records such as the *Luoyang Jialan Ji* mention a monk named Damo—the Chinese name for Bodhidharma—who arrived at the Shaolin monastery. While his primary mission was to propagate Chan (Zen) Buddhism, he is also believed to have introduced physical training techniques that later evolved into the Shaolin martial arts tradition. These cross-cultural connections highlight how widely Indian martial traditions were believed to have travelled and evolved. Kalaripayattu itself represents a highly sophisticated system of combat that integrates agile body movements, breath control, and meditative postures, thereby strengthening both body and mind. The word Kalari means 'training ground' or simply 'place of learning.' This name is significant, for the ancient Indians regarded martial training as an essential component of education and personal growth. Children who completed their foundational studies at local gurukulams—hermitage schools conducted by sages—would join their village Kalari for advanced physical and military training. In fact, mastery of Kalari was a lifelong pursuit and continued well into adulthood.

Moreover, in ancient India, Kalari was open to all, irrespective of gender or socio-economic background. Girls trained alongside boys, and even in single combat practise they were matched against one another to test endurance and skill. In other words, within the Kalari system, one was not defined as a man or a woman, but simply as a warrior.

In the next section, we will take a closer look at the disciplined training system of the Kalari, highlighting its rituals, physical conditioning, healing practices, and the progressive mastery of weapons and combat techniques.

Body, Weapon, and Wisdom: The Training Tradition of the Kalari

Training in the ancient martial tradition was guided by discipline, ritual, and a deep awareness of the body and its environment. Every aspect of practice—from daily routines to the design of the training space—was carefully structured to cultivate both physical skill and mental focus.

The training for Kalari began at dawn. No one entered the training space—also known as Kalari—without bathing and changing into the prescribed training attire, typically a tightly draped loincloth for boys, and a loincloth with a chest drape for girls. The training spaces were constructed in accordance with the guidelines of Vastu Shastra and strict architectural principles. Their design ensured proper lighting and ventilation while creating an environment conducive to disciplining both body and mind. Even the flooring reflected this thoughtful approach as it was layered with red earth mixed with Ayurvedic herbs, which helped soothe and heal the minor cuts and injuries that often occurred during practice.

A notable point is that in earlier times, nearly every village had its own Kalari, presided over by a deity, often Bhagavathy, the divine feminine, revered as protector and source of strength. Each morning, before training commenced, the students and the guru offered salutations to the presiding deity. They applied the *tilakam* on their own foreheads and on the idol of the deity using soil from the Kalari ground. The first act symbolised humility and the surrendering of ego; the second signified the unity of the human and the divine, joined through the element of earth.

Kalari training commenced with rigorous exercises designed to cultivate immense strength and exceptional flexibility. Students also underwent therapeutic oil massages to enhance suppleness and treat muscular strain. Unlike conventional massages performed solely by hand, Kalari massage often involves the use of the feet. The guru, supported by ropes suspended from the ceiling, skilfully applied controlled pressure with his feet on vital points of the trainee's body in smooth, flowing movements. Such a refined practice required an intimate knowledge of human anatomy. Consequently, Kalari students were educated not only in martial techniques but also in anatomy and aspects of medicine that today would fall under sports medicine. In this sense, every Kalari warrior was, in his or her own right, a practitioner of combat as well as healing.

Unlike many other martial art systems in the world, Kalari teaches weapon-based techniques first, and bare-handed combat last. This sequencing is deliberate as it builds a strong foundation of body control, flexibility, rhythm, and spatial awareness before transitioning to unarmed techniques. Weapons training refines body mechanics and muscle memory, both of which are essential for effective combat. Handling weapons with reach, such as spears or swords, demands an acute awareness of one's surroundings and the opponent's position. This cultivated spatial intelligence is later applied to bare-handed combat, where the practitioner learns to anticipate attacks and respond with precision. The ultimate aspiration was to reach a level where the weapon became an extension of one's own limb.

The weapons used in Kalari include maces, spears, daggers, swords, and the *urumi* (a ribbon-like, flexible sword that requires exceptional mastery). With a single swing, the urumi can inflict multiple cuts on an opponent, and if mishandled, on the wielder as well.

The use of such weapons was only one aspect of a far more elaborate training system that shaped the Kalari practitioner. Kalari training progresses through eighteen levels, attained gradually by the most disciplined and resilient students over several years. In addition, there are eight foundational postures or stances, each inspired by careful observation of animals and their distinctive anatomical strengths:

1. *Gaja vadivu* (elephant posture)
2. *Ashwa vadivu* (horse posture)
3. *Simha vadivu* (lion posture)

4. *Varaaha vadivu* (wild boar posture)
5. *Kukkuda vadivu* (rooster posture)
6. *Sarpa vadivu* (snake posture)
7. *Matsya vadivu* (fish posture)
8. *Marjara vadivu* (cat posture)

Other than this, one of the most extraordinary dimensions of Kalari is its application of *Marma Shastra* (the science of striking vital points). It is said that accomplished warriors could disable, or even kill, an opponent by striking the correct *marma* with their fingers. Through careful study of the human body, ancient Kalari masters identified numerous vital points in the human body which, when struck, could cause paralysis, loss of consciousness, muscular stiffening, or death. Such knowledge was imparted only to the most mature and level-headed disciples to prevent misuse.

The earliest reference to marmam appears in the Rigveda, which narrates how Indra defeated Vritra by attacking his vital point. Later, Sushruta, in the *Sushruta Samhita*, composed around 600 BCE, classified 107 vital points in the human body, of which sixty-four were considered lethal if struck with a fist or stick. Significantly, *Marma Shastra*, emerging from the Ayurvedic tradition, was not confined to combat. The same knowledge of vital points was used therapeutically in marma treatment to heal injuries and restore balance.

Another significant aspect of Kalari is that although it cultivates strength, agility, flexibility, and dexterity, it also places equal emphasis on unwavering focus and keen observation. This enables the practitioner to anticipate an opponent's next move. And despite being a martial discipline, its fundamental teaching is self-control. It rests on the principle that only the weak and insecure are easily agitated. One who is confident in one's strength resorts to force only when there is no other option. For this reason, Kalari training includes sustained periods of meditation and introspection.

Perhaps this inner dimension explains why the monks of the Shaolin monastery could integrate such techniques into their disciplined lifestyle, for Kalari offers a method to mould and master both body and mind.

From a societal perspective, Kalari also served as a means to minimise war-related deaths. When two kingdoms or villages entered into conflict, an alternative to mass warfare was sometimes proposed. Each side would nominate a highly skilled Kalari warrior to represent them. Instead of entire armies clashing and causing hundreds or thousands of deaths, these chosen warriors would engage in a decisive duel.

Even in moments of conflict, the tradition upheld a striking degree of dignity and autonomy for the warrior. Unlike many traditions where rulers imposed their choice, in the Kalari system, the king or chieftain formally visited the warrior's home, requested his/her representation, and awaited his/her consent. The decision to participate rested entirely with the warrior. Thus, in order to save the lives of their fellow people, these brave individuals voluntarily risked their own, for in a Kalaripayattu duel, only the victor returned alive.

It is also worth noting that the Kalari warriors of ancient India were celebrated as heroes. Bards sang of their bravery and adventure, carrying their heroic tales to neighbouring cities and kingdoms. Among these legends were stories of formidable women warriors who fought valiantly and defeated countless men in combat.

Kalari was also not merely a system of offence and defence; it was a disciplined path to self-confidence, self-mastery, and the development of a strong personality. The guru often encouraged friendly combat between students to give them first-hand experience of real confrontation. And when such matches occasionally grew intense or aggressive, the vigilant guru would intervene, halt the duel, make the students hold each other's hands, and ask them to say, 'I forgive, and I forget.' In this simple yet powerful ritual lay a profound lesson: the warrior must never be overpowered by emotion. The fight is against the opponent's moves, not against the opponent. In this way, deep philosophy and spirituality were seamlessly infused into the fighting tradition.

Together, these traditions reveal that Kalari was far more than a battlefield discipline. It was a moral and philosophical system that cultivated courage, restraint, and a deep sense of responsibility towards society. In shaping warriors who were both formidable and self-controlled, it ensured that strength was guided by wisdom and honour.

The Kalari Way: A Path to Strength and Growth

As we have seen, ancient Indians placed great importance on cultivating a strong and flexible body capable of supporting a balanced and disciplined mind, enabling individuals to navigate life with confidence and self-control. Kalari formed an essential part of this holistic vision. Moreover, it was not reserved solely for aspiring warriors or soldiers but was open to anyone who sought to live with discipline, purpose, and inner strength. And while the outward movements of Kalari appear vigorous and even fierce, the practitioner is trained to maintain an inner state of calmness and composure. Over time, with meditation and devotion to the divine feminine woven into its training, Kalari evolved beyond a mere system of combat into a spiritual discipline. The early morning practice sessions further reinforced this purpose, awakening the body, revitalising the senses, and filling the practitioner with renewed energy for the day ahead.

Today, we often read about children facing challenges and vulnerabilities in many spaces, both private and public. While awareness of potential dangers is important, the ability to defend oneself is equally vital. This makes it worthwhile to consider introducing foundational Kalari training alongside formal school education. With thoughtful planning at the administrative level, such an initiative could be implemented without imposing a financial burden on parents.

Learning Kalari could help children grow into well-rounded individuals who are strong not only in body but also in character.

One can imagine a generation equipped with physical capability and mental resilience to move through life with strength, balance, and a winner's attitude.

Takeaways from the Ancient Past

- Recognising the importance of learning a martial art from childhood, not only to build physical strength but also to cultivate a mature and well-rounded personality, encourages the development of restraint, resilience, and clarity of mind through disciplined training and meditation.
- Teaching combat techniques alongside detailed knowledge of human anatomy and the treatment of injuries highlights the value of integrating skill with responsibility.
- Blending spirituality with an inherently aggressive art form instils righteousness and devotion, enabling the practitioner to approach combat as a duty while keeping emotions such as hatred, anger, and enmity at bay.

Chapter 14

ANIMALS AND CARE

'He who sees all beings in the self and the self in all beings, loses all vestige of fear.'

—Isha Upanishad

Pashu: Animal Keeping in Ancient India

By now, you know the extent to which the ancient Indians went to take care of themselves as individuals and nurture themselves as a community. This spirit of care did not end with the human community. Their concern and compassion extended to the flora and fauna that thrived around them. Beyond their spiritual and ecological significance as fellow living beings, animals and birds played a vital role in the daily life of ancient Indians.

Archaeological evidence shows that animal keeping, or domestication, was active in the Indian subcontinent as early as 8,000 years ago. The people of the Indus Valley Civilisation domesticated ibex, dogs, cats, bulls, stags, cows, sheep, goats, buffaloes, fowls, and elephants. The famous seal of the humped bull is one among many artefacts that throw light on the animal-keeping culture of ancient India.

Moreover, cattle husbandry was highly developed during the Rigvedic period. The ancient Indians also studied animal anatomy and physiology in great detail. The Atharva Veda contains sections that discuss various animal diseases along with their treatment methods, healing herbs, and medicinal preparations. Also, the Mahabharata mentions that the twin princes Nakula and Sahadeva were experts in animal healthcare. Nakula, an authority on horses, authored *Ashva Chikitsa*, a treatise on the care and treatment of horses, while Sahadeva specialised in the management and health of cattle.

Shalihotra, a veterinarian and author who lived in the third century BCE, is regarded as the founder of veterinary science. He spent his entire life documenting and studying animal life and healthcare. Living in the illustrious city of Sravasti in present-day Uttar Pradesh, he wrote an encyclopaedic treatise on the healthcare and management of horses called *Shalihotra Samhita*. Containing 12,000 shlokas, this remarkable work has been translated into English, Arabic, Iranian, and Tibetan. The text provides elaborate details on horse anatomy, physiology, diseases affecting equine species, treatment methods, and even surgical interventions. It also describes the distinctive features of various breeds of horses and explains the qualities to look for when selecting an ideal horse.

Horses also played a central role in the royal ritual known as *ashvamedha*. It was an ingenious way of expanding a king's territory without immediately resorting to violence. A horse chosen by the king and the royal priest was allowed to roam freely through neighbouring lands. Kings who accepted the sovereignty of the sender king paid their respects to the horse and thus became vassal rulers. Those who wished to challenge the king would stop and tie the horse, which led to war. In this way, the horse became a symbolic instrument in a remarkably strategic approach to peace and power.

Another significant work, *Hasti Ayurveda*, written by the sage Palakapya around 500 BCE, is an extensive text devoted entirely to elephants. Written in the form of a dialogue between Lomapada, the king of Anga, and the sage Palakapya, the text explores the natural habitat of elephants, methods of capturing and taming them, legends associated with them, their diet and lifestyle, as well as their anatomy, diseases, and treatment methods.

The text also narrates that the kingdom of Anga once suffered severe agricultural damage due to frequent incursions by wild elephants. Crops were repeatedly destroyed, and farmers faced enormous losses. It was at this difficult moment that Palakapya devised systematic methods to tame elephants. At the same time, he emphasised humane practices, insisting that the methods should enable humans and elephants to coexist without harming one another. Palakapya himself was known to be deeply fond of elephants, and his work reflects this compassion.

It likewise merits attention that ancient India had veterinary hospitals more than 3,000 years ago, making them arguably among the earliest medical facilities for animals in the world. Archaeological evidence also suggests that Emperor Ashoka generously supported the establishment of animal care centres across the Indian subcontinent. His rock edicts, particularly Rock Edict II and V, clearly mention provisions for medical care for both humans and animals. One such inscription states:

'Everywhere within the dominions of the beloved of the gods (Ashoka), and in the lands beyond the borders—the Cholas, the Pandyas, the Satyaputras, the Keralaputras, and as far as Tamraparni (Sri Lanka)—the beloved of the gods has arranged for two types of medical treatment: medical treatment for humans and medical treatment for animals.'

These hospitals for animals were surrounded by protective walls and divided into separate sections where different species or categories of animals and birds were housed and treated. Interestingly, some of these facilities even had wards for creatures that we today consider pests, such as mice and rats, as well as animals one might not expect to receive medical attention in ancient times, such as tortoises.

This intriguing detail points towards two possibilities. On the one hand, the people of ancient India may have been extraordinarily compassionate animal lovers who cared even for creatures that others tend to disregard. On the other, it suggests that people kept a wide variety of animals as companions, ranging from mice to tortoises.

Surgeries were also performed in these hospitals, and such procedures may have been practised as early as the Vedic period. Skilled vaidyas carried out animal surgeries with remarkable precision. Detailed descriptions of surgical techniques and instruments can be found in the works of Shalihotra and Palakapya, further demonstrating the advanced level of veterinary knowledge that existed in ancient India.

All these accounts reveal that compassion for living beings in ancient India extended far beyond human society. Care for animals was institutionalised through organised hospitals, medical treatments, and even surgical practices. Such traditions reflect a worldview in which all forms of life were regarded as worthy of protection and healing.

Sacred Companions: Domestic and Divine Animals in Ancient Indian Society

Animals occupied a meaningful place in the cultural and spiritual imagination of ancient India. Many species were not only domesticated but also absorbed into mythology, symbolism, and daily life.

Of all the animals in ancient India, the most important was the cow. The zebu (Indicine cattle or humped cattle) was considered sacred. Seals, idols, motifs, and statues of the zebu cow and bull have been excavated from sites ranging from the Indus Valley to Ashokan pillars and Indo-Scythian coins. The Mahabharata says that cows should be treated with the same respect as one's mother. In fact, the ancient Indians called her '*gomata*' (the cow mother). Yaska, a seventh-century linguist and etymologist, who explained many difficult words from the Rigveda through his great etymological text *Nirukta*, gives nine names and meanings for the cow from the Rigveda. The first name is *aghanya*, meaning 'the unslayable' or that which should not be slaughtered. Even the earliest Buddhist text, *Sutta Nipata*, eloquently describes the cow as the giver of food (*annada*), beauty (*vannada*), and happiness (*sukhada*).

This veneration of the cow was not a superstition but a reflection of the deep spiritual connection human beings felt with every animal in the world. From the Vedic times, cows enriched the lives of the people through milk, butter, curd, and ghee as nourishment, cow dung and urine for agriculture, and even in death, their skin was used to make percussion instruments. For this reason, the ancient Indians saw the cow as a symbol of selfless giving, gentle care, and boundless abundance.

Apart from cows, dogs were also widely domesticated from the time of the Indus Valley Civilisation and held a distinctive place in ancient Indian society. The Rigveda mentions Indra's celestial female dog Sarama, who is the divine progenitor of all canines. Known as Devashuni (the dog of the gods), this companion of Indra helped him recover the divine cows stolen by the Panis, indicating her loyalty and importance to the gods. Yama, the god of death, has two dogs named Sharvara and Shyama who guard the gates of *naraka* (the underworld). They are identified with the constellations Canis Major and Canis Minor respectively. Additionally, the word Sharvara means variegated or spotted, and the word Shyama means black or dark-coloured. These fierce guardians watch the gates and scrutinise departed souls before they enter the underworld. This reflects how ancient Indians recognised the remarkable ability of dogs to sense wrongdoing and detect crimes.

The Mahabharata itself ends with the story of a dog, when Yudhishtira refuses to enter heaven without his loyal companion who accompanies him during his final journey. God Dattatreya's four dogs symbolise the four Vedas, the ultimate source of knowledge. Can you think of any other time or culture in history where dogs have been used as symbols of ultimate cosmic knowledge?

Aside from this, cats were also depicted in unique and interesting ways in ancient India. Shashti, the goddess of fertility and child protection, is often portrayed as cat-faced or riding a giant cat, because cats were associated with fertility. In the Mahabharata, there is a symbolic story of Lomasha the cat, who engages in a deep philosophical conversation with Patila the mouse on the subject of escaping death. In the Ramayana, Indra, after secretly seducing Ahalya, escapes the hermitage disguised as a cat, because cats symbolised stealth. The *Dharma Shastras* and the *Dharma Sutras* condemn harming or killing cats and describe the process of expiation or atonement for such a crime. Additionally, at sites of the Indus Valley Civilisation, archaeologists have discovered paw prints of cats on bricks over 4,000 years old, quietly preserving evidence of their long-standing companionship with the people of ancient India.

Interestingly, one of the Sanskrit words for cat is *marjara*, derived from the root word *mrij*, meaning 'to cleanse.' The cat is perhaps called marjara because of its habit of constantly grooming and cleansing itself.

Another important fact is that the ancient Indians connected each of their gods and goddesses with an animal or bird, as a steed or companion. Krishna was a cowherd, and he loved and was loved by all animals and birds. When he played his flute, all the animals and birds—herbivores and carnivores alike—gathered around him, mesmerised by the magnetic music and forgetting their predator-prey roles. This beautifully shows how music and love can unite an entire ecosystem, and how such harmony itself is divine.

Shiva's steed is the bull Nandi, reflecting his brute power and ferocity. Lakshmi, the goddess of wealth and prosperity, is associated with the owl, symbolising the importance of being observant even in dark times, and also reminding us that too much wealth can blur our vision about truth even in bright light. Vishnu sleeps upon a thousand-headed serpent in his cosmic slumber, symbolising the thousand perspectives that ultimately unite in a single meditative truth.

Furthermore, the ancient spiritual texts say that Lord Vishnu, the ultimate preserver of the universe, incarnated on earth ten times across vast eons as Matsya (the fish), Kurma (the turtle), Varaha (the boar), Narasimha (the half beast, half human), Vamana (the miniature human), Parashurama (the axe wielder), Rama (the bearer of the bow and arrow), Balarama (the wielder of the plough), Krishna (the philosopher), and in the future Kalki (the destroyer of darkness). Through these trans-eonic incarnations, the ancient Indians were conveying two profound ideas. First, that the pulsating presence of the divine exists in all forms of life, including animals. Second, that life on earth itself evolved through stages: from the aquatic, to the amphibian, to the terrestrial, to the primitive primate, to the early human, to the crude weapon user, to the archer, to the agriculturalist, to the artist-thinker, and finally to a future possibility of a universal cleanser. In this way, our genius ancestors were showing that all of us—modern and civilised as we believe ourselves to be—belong to the same primordial consciousness.

A notable point here is that right from the Vedic period, the ancient Indians called for *ahimsa* (non-violence or non-injury) towards all bipeds and quadrupeds, equating harm to any life with the highest and most heinous crime. This principle goes beyond mere vegetarianism and rests on seeing the divine in every living being. Hymn 8.3.25 of the Atharva Veda condemns all killing, including that of humans, cattle, and horses, and prays to Agni, the god of fire, to punish those who commit such acts. It is noteworthy that by invoking Agni, they perhaps implied not merely physical punishment but the purification of the mind. In other words, the true punishment was the cleansing of one's mindset so that human beings could live and coexist harmoniously with the diverse fauna around them.

Living Symbols: Animals as Teachers of Values and Virtue

The ancient Indians were both a pantheistic and a panentheistic culture. They saw the divine in animals and animals within the divine. Just as all forms of energy contribute to the balance of the universe, animal energy, too, was considered essential for maintaining that balance. In no other culture in the history of the world do we find a society that unanimously declared an animal to be unslayable and worthy of reverence like one's own mother. In fact, every animal represented a value that the ancient Indians aspired to cultivate within themselves.

This highlights how, on one level, animals were kept for agriculture, livelihood, and other practical needs. But on a deeper level, they helped nurture a culture grounded in universal love and mutual respect for every living being. That is why the ancient Indians embedded their highest texts of knowledge and spirituality with stories, practices, and values that emphasised reverence for animals.

The significance of this bond with animals is now being reinforced by modern science. Being around animals and forming connections with them has been shown to uplift mood and provide emotional support, even for those struggling with depression. In ancient India, people spent meaningful time with the animals in their households and cared for them with devotion. The emotional and spiritual support this fostered was remarkable. This reverence is evident in the common morning practice of bathing the cow and expressing gratitude for her selfless generosity. In this way, the cow became an elegant symbol for all animals that form part of a delicate and interconnected ecosystem.

Today, we may not begin our day by bathing an animal, but we can start with a small gesture, such as feeding an animal, donating even a small amount to an animal care home, volunteering an hour each month, or simply offering a moment of mental gratitude to the countless creatures that sustain and enrich our natural world.

Takeaways from the Ancient Past

- Loving and revering domesticated animals for the nourishment, comfort, and protection they provide encourages gratitude towards fellow living beings and fosters happiness and peace of mind.
- Adopting a vegetarian diet grounded in the principle of ahimsa reflects non-injury and universal love, showing that dietary choices can nurture both health and a deeper spirituality.
- Studying and developing healthcare practices for different species of domesticated animals highlights the recognition of each animal as unique, with its own needs, and teaches us to approach care with attention and responsibility.

Chapter 15

MOON AND SLEEP

'Just as in the waking state the external objects are perceived, so also in the dream state the internal impressions are seen.'
—Mandukya Karika

Chandra: The Ever-Changing Moon

In ancient India, celestial bodies were not merely objects of observation but held deep spiritual and cultural significance. While the sun governed the day, the moon shaped rituals, timekeeping, and philosophical reflections during the night.

The earliest work on astrology in India is the *Vedanga Jyotisha*, compiled around 3,200 years ago. Additionally, the Atharva Veda, compiled around 3,100 years ago, gives detailed descriptions of the moon and other planetary bodies. The moon was called Chandra in Sanskrit, meaning 'bright,' 'shining,' or 'glittering.' Ancient texts mention that Chandra is illuminated at night by the light of Surya, the sun god, revealing how advanced their astronomical understanding was. The moon was also associated with the gentle and nurturing feminine aspect of energy within the body and was believed to bring a sense of peace. Its phases were seen as symbolic of the cyclical nature of life, reflecting the continual rhythms of birth, death, and rebirth.

The *Purusha Sukta*, an important section of the Rigveda, says:

> '*Chandrama Manaso Jaatah*
> *Chaksho Suryo Ajaayata.*'
>
> (Chandra, the moon, is born from the mind, and Surya, the sun, from the eyes of the primordial being.)

This idea suggests that during the day, one perceives the external world through the eyes, while during the night, one perceives the self through the mind. So, when the ancient Indians said that Chandra influences the human mind and emotions, they were also indicating that the best time for introspection and self-analysis is the night, when one is free from the chores, duties, and distractions of the day. Moreover, the waxing and waning of the moon were compared to the unpredictable and ever-changing nature of the human mind. At night, when one rests and the outer world quietens, the mind becomes active and wanders in many directions. It is at this time that one is encouraged to look inward and bring stability to the fluttering mind.

However, if you think that the ancient Indians focused only on the spiritual and symbolic nature of the moon, you are in for a surprise. From the time of the Vedic scholars, the moon was carefully studied from a scientific and astronomical perspective. Among the many ancient Indian texts on astronomy, the *Surya Siddhanta*, compiled over 1,600 years ago, provides detailed information about the moon and several other planetary bodies. It calculates the sidereal period of the moon—the time the moon takes to complete one orbit around the earth as measured against distant stars—as 27.322 days while the modern value is 27.32166 days. The text also discusses in detail the rising and setting of the moon, its cusps, its dimensions, and eclipses.

The ancient Indians divided every month into two lunar phases: the *shukla paksha* and the *krishna paksha*. The shukla paksha, or the white phase, is the waxing phase of the moon, while the krishna paksha, or the dark phase, is the waning phase. *Poornima*, or the full moon, held the greatest significance because it is the time when the moon shines in its fullest brilliance. It was, therefore, considered the best time of the month for introspective and spiritual practices at night.

The reverence for the full moon was so profound that the ancient Indians celebrated *shatabhishekam* when a person had witnessed one thousand poornimas in their lifetime. This milestone is reached when one enters the eighty-first year of life. Shatabhishekam symbolises emotional maturity, wisdom, and the fullness of a life lived with experience.

Another popular practise at the time for balancing the body and mind during the night was a sequence of yogic postures, movements, and breathing techniques called Chandra Namaskaram, or the moon salutation. It served as the counterpart to Surya Namaskaram and was practised in the evening when the moon was visible. Known for its cooling and soothing effects, it helped calm the mind and foster a sense of serenity.

It is also noteworthy that ancient Indians typically had their dinner early, either before or just after sunset. Following their evening prayers, family members would often gather in the front or inner courtyard of the house under the moonlight. In a joint family setting, grandparents, parents, children, and grandchildren sat together in a large circle around the eldest member of the household. During these gatherings, they shared the stories of their day, discussed challenges, and explored possible solutions while listening to the guidance and wisdom of their elders. This practice fostered a profound sense of security, as everyone knew they had a supportive network to rely on in times of difficulty. In many ways, these nightly conversations served a healing and cathartic role similar to what we today recognise as group therapy or counselling.

Thus, after the evening bath, temple darsanam, the practice of Chandra Namaskaram, family discussions, and moments of quiet introspection, an individual would gradually attain a state of relaxed harmony between body and mind. Only then was the ancient Indian ready to retire for the night, entering the *shayana griham*, the sleeping chamber.

Nidra: The Mystical Sleep

Nidra, or sleep, fascinated the ancient Indians from the earliest phases of their civilisation. They sought to understand the process of sleep and the mysterious realm into which human consciousness enters during rest. Research shows that sleep was studied thousands of years ago, and knowledge about it began to be systematically compiled at least 3,000 years ago in the Atharva Veda. The Mandukya Upanishad and the Prashna Upanishad explore the theme of sleep, its cycles, and its patterns in remarkable depth. Ayurveda also emphasises the significance of sleep and considers night sleep extremely important, stating that 'night sleep nurses all living beings.' It also warns against *nidraadhikya*, or excessive sleep, and *asvapna*, or insomnia, both of which are regarded as unhealthy conditions.

In addition, Ayurveda classifies seven types of sleep based on their causative factors. According to it, sleep can arise from physiological, psychological, or pathological causes. The seven types of sleep that fall under these categories are:

- Sleep produced as a result of night-time (physiological).
- Sleep due to tamas (ignorance). This type of sleep leads to errors in thought and action.
- Sleep due to an imbalance of the *kapha dhatu*, which is one of the three humours of the body.
- Sleep caused by mental exertion.
- Sleep caused by physical exertion.
- Sleep caused by the bad prognosis of a disease.
- Sleep caused as a side effect of a disease (for example, fever).

Another text that examines sleep from an Ayurvedic and lifestyle perspective is the *Charaka Samhita*, compiled over 2,600 years ago. Describing the process of falling asleep, Charaka states, 'When the mind becomes tired, and the senses grow dull and incapable of functioning, the person goes to sleep.' He further explains that proper sleep leads to happiness and longevity. An important point to note is that, although the text classifies dreams into seven types, Charaka does not place much emphasis on their meanings, viewing them instead as natural expressions of the sleeping mind. These classifications are outlined below.

- Dreams about objects seen earlier.
- Dreams about things heard earlier.
- Dreams about past experiences.
- Dreams arising from wish fulfilment.
- Dreams created by imagination.
- Premonitory dreams.
- Dreams about morbid or disturbing things.

Some other notable texts that explore the nature of dreams are the Mandukya Upanishad, which states, 'When the mind withdraws from sense objects, the dream state begins, and the self creates a world of its own,' and the *Sushruta Samhita*, which devotes an entire chapter to dream analysis. Sushruta notes that every dream, whether major or minor, reveals something about the state of the body or the mind. Besides this, great pioneers of medicine such as Vagbhatta also wrote extensively about dreams.

Considering the depth of research and the range of insights and analyses developed thousands of years ago, it is remarkable that ancient thinkers observed, studied, and wrote about phenomena as subtle and elusive as sleep and dreams. These reflections reveal the extraordinary curiosity of the ancient mind, which had already begun exploring the mysterious inner world of human consciousness long before the rise of modern psychology and neuroscience.

The Art of Sleeping Well: Nightly Discipline in Ancient India

In ancient Indian medical thought, sleep was not viewed as a passive act but as an important pillar of health. Great attention was therefore given not only to the duration of sleep but also to posture and habits that could support the body's natural processes during the night.

Ancient Indians viewed sleep as a divine presence and called it Nidra Devi, the goddess of sleep, a nurturing feminine force that gently carried human consciousness through the realms of sleep, dream, and deep sleep towards relaxation and rejuvenation. And to honour this sacred presence and prepare themselves for restful sleep, they followed a carefully designed nightly routine rooted in both physical and mental discipline.

This practice began even before entering the bedroom. The ancient Indians would wash their feet, hands, and face, cleansing themselves after the day's activities. They would then sit quietly in the bedroom and meditate for a short while as a way of preparing the mind for sleep. After the day's work, temple darsanam, Chandra Namaskaram, and meditation, the body and mind had been fully engaged and were ready to rest and relax.

Another notable point is that they sought to cleanse not only the body but also the mind before going to bed, so that the divine goddess would make their eyelids heavy and bless them with deep sleep. They would then lie down, close their eyes, reflect upon the thoughts and actions of the day, and softly chant the following mantra before drifting into sleep:

'Kara charana kritam vaak-kaayajam vaa
Shravana nayanajam vaa maanasam vaaparaadham
Vihitam avihitam vaa
Sarvame tat kshamasva.'

(All the errors and wrongs I committed through my hands and feet, through my body and words, through my ears and eyes, and through my mind, for those actions which are prescribed and also for those which are not prescribed and done through my own free will, for all of them, please forgive me.)

Another aspect that received careful attention was the posture one adopted during sleep. And although any comfortable body position may be considered suitable for sleep, lying on one's right side, known as *dakshinashayana*, is regarded as the ideal position. This is because the stomach and pancreas lie more towards the left side of the body. Sleeping on the right side allows gravity to assist digestion by helping the stomach contents move more easily into the intestines. This position also prevents unnecessary pressure on the heart and stomach and promotes better digestion overnight. Aside from this, improper sleep and diet were considered major causes of both obesity and emaciation. Ayurveda, therefore, prescribes various treatments and herbal preparations to regulate both the duration and quality of sleep.

All this highlights the fact that the ancient Indians placed great importance on uninterrupted and restorative sleep, recognising it as essential not only for the body's renewal but also for the mind's clarity and spiritual growth. By approaching rest with such awareness, they ensured that sleep became a vital part of a balanced and harmonious life.

The Four States of Awareness: Insights from the Mandukya Upanishad

As seen earlier, sleep and dreams fascinated the ancient Indians, but an important reason for this fascination was that they placed consciousness at the very centre of their inquiry. This deep interest in consciousness also found expression in the way ancient texts carefully described its different states. The Mandukya Upanishad speaks of four states of consciousness: *jagrat*, *svapna*, *sushupti*, and *turiya*. Let's take a closer look.

Jagrat refers to the waking state, when consciousness is in contact with the objects of the external world. Svapna, which also means dream, is the dream state in which mental images arise from memory or imagination. In this state, the person is not considered fully asleep. Sushupti resembles the state of dreamless sleep, where there are no mental images and the mind becomes completely blank. The Brihadaranyaka Upanishad beautifully describes this state: 'As a person in the arms of the beloved is unaware of what is outside and what is within, so a person in deep sleep is unaware of desire or dream.'

Lastly, turiya, which literally means 'the fourth,' is the highest state of consciousness, where the individual experiences union with ultimate reality. As the *Yoga Vasishta* declares, 'As the ocean remains unchanged though waves rise and fall, so is turiya, unaffected by waking, dreaming, or deep sleep.' Additionally, the yogis of ancient India believed that a person naturally transcends the first three states of consciousness upon attaining the sublime state of turiya.

Together, these ideas reveal how profoundly ancient Indian thinkers explored the inner landscape of the mind. Their examination of consciousness shows a philosophical depth that continues to intrigue scholars even today.

Pause before Sleep: Reflection and Renewal at Night

In the ancient Indian understanding of daily life, the transition from day to night was not merely a change of time but a shift in rhythm and awareness. As the sun set and daylight gradually yielded to the soft glow of the moon, life naturally moved towards stillness and introspection. While the daytime was devoted to physically and mentally demanding activities, the night was meant for recovery, allowing the body and mind to restore their lost energy and vitality. Recognising the profound importance of deep and undisturbed sleep for both immediate renewal and long-term physical and mental stability, ancient Indians incorporated thoughtful practices into their nightly routines to prepare themselves for restful slumber.

One such simple yet meaningful practice involved a brief moment of reflection before sleep. Once in bed, individuals would quietly review the actions of the day and seek forgiveness from

God, time, nature, or the universe for anything they felt had been inappropriate. This gentle act of self-examination served as a form of inner cleansing, helping them release the burdens of the day while cultivating awareness and a sincere resolve to improve. And in today's world, where many struggle to obtain proper rest and often rely on sleep aids, reviving such mindful practices may offer a natural path to calmer nights and more refreshing mornings.

Takeaways from the Ancient Past

- Eating a light dinner shortly after sunset so that the food is digested and the stomach can relax by bedtime encourages the body and mind to prepare for deep and restorative sleep.
- Practising Chandra Namaskaram, the yogic sequence associated with the cooling and calming qualities of the moon, stretches the muscles, soothes the mind, and prepares the body for a restful night's sleep.
- Gathering together as a family at night to share the events of the day and seek guidance from elders encourages open communication and creates a supportive space for resolving concerns.
- Washing the body, practising a brief meditation, and reflecting on the day's thoughts and actions before sleep cultivates inner peace and allows one to rest with a clear and calm mind.

Chapter 16

DEATH AND BEYOND

'The soul leaves the body at death just as a guest leaves an inn without attachment.'

—Mahabharata

Mrtyu: The Philosophical Vision of Death in Ancient India

In the ancient Indian worldview, life was always understood in relation to a deeper spiritual reality. This perspective shaped not only their understanding of health and consciousness but also their reflections on mortality. And while they documented extensive knowledge to safeguard the well-being of the body and mind, the ancient Indians consistently regarded the mind—and the deeper self beyond it—as more fundamental than the physical body. From this standpoint, *mrtyu* (death) was not viewed merely as a tragic end, but as the final relinquishment of the body within a larger cosmic journey. It is therefore not surprising that some of the earliest recorded reflections on death are found in ancient India, particularly in the hymns of the Rigveda, where the mystery of life and its inevitable conclusion is contemplated with remarkable philosophical depth.

One such hymn, referred to as 'The Song of Creation', declares, 'Death was not there. Nor was there anything immortal. The world was a total void, except for one thing, breathless, yet breathed by its own nature.' And while this hymn reflects on the origin of creation and the self-born divine, its reference to mrtyu subtly conveys a deeper idea: that birth and death are not opposing realities, but complementary aspects of the same cosmic truth. In this vision, life and death emerge as two expressions of a single, continuous process of existence.

Several other notable texts further expand the breadth and depth with which death was studied in ancient India, examining it not only as a biological event but also as a profound spiritual and philosophical transition.

1. The *Bhagavata Purana* states, 'For one who has taken birth in a body, death has also appeared. Whether today or a hundred years later, the death of all living beings is certain.' This statement underscores the inevitability of death and encourages the cultivation of acceptance towards it.

2. The *Yoga Vasishta* approaches death from a radically rational and philosophical perspective: 'If death is the end of everything and there is no life after death, can anything be more beneficial than that? Because one gets completely freed from all kinds of worldly sorrows once and for all. It is said that on relinquishing an old body, new life is bestowed in a new body. In reality, a new birth after death may occur or may not occur. Either way, death is a happy event.' Such a view makes the idea of death accessible even to those who may not believe in God, spirituality, or rebirth, for the argument rests on a pragmatic and logical foundation.

3. The Bhagavad Gita presents death in compassionate terms: 'Death is as loving and giving as a mother. It takes you under its wings irrespective of whether you venerate, worship, or remember it.' While acknowledging death as an unavoidable

reality, this perspective also highlights its impartial and universal nature.

4. In ancient Indian thought, death was broadly classified into two categories, namely, *akaala mrtyu* (untimely death) and *kaala mrtyu* (natural death). However, the Atharva Veda refers to as many as 101 forms of akaala mrtyu, including death caused by accidents, poison, illness, suicide, and war. It also suggests that such untimely deaths may sometimes be prevented through medicines, *rasayanas*, mantras, yoga, and certain specialised practices. Natural death, however, was understood to be inevitable.

   Additionally, ancient texts describe this natural end with poetic simplicity: 'In old age, the strength of the *prana* (life force), the body, and its organs gradually decline, and death arrives gently, like a dry leaf falling from a tree.'

To summarise, these reflections reveal that ancient Indian thinkers approached death not with fear, but with clarity, acceptance, and philosophical depth. In their view, death was not the negation of life, but a natural transition within the larger rhythm of existence.

The Rhythm of Existence: Time, Soul, and the Meaning of Death

When we look at the attitude that ancient Indians had towards death, one key observation stands out. Their understanding of death was closely intertwined with deeper philosophical ideas about time, the self, and the nature of existence. These insights helped people view mortality not with fear, but with understanding and acceptance. To understand this perspective more clearly, it is essential to see how they explained death within the larger framework of time itself.

The ancient seers of India taught that death is a natural and inevitable movement within the larger flow of time, ensuring that it was neither feared nor resisted. For this reason, the god of death was called Kala—a term that also signifies 'time'—

emphasising that death is not an isolated event but an integral part of life's continuous unfolding. This understanding was rooted in a profound conception of the self: while the body is temporary, the soul endures, untouched by the passage of time.

In contrast to the linear view of time common in Western thought, the ancient Indians saw time as eternal and cyclical. Past, present, and future were interconnected, each shaping and influencing the others, forming an unbroken stream of existence. Within this cyclical framework, life and death are inseparable, two facets of the same cosmic rhythm. By recognising that Kala, whether understood as time or death, impacts only the body and never the soul, the ancient thinkers offered a perspective in which the fear of death could be transcended, allowing life to be lived with courage, clarity, and inner freedom.

In addition to this view, the body was seen merely as a vehicle carrying the jivatman, the individual soul that experiences life through a particular body and mind and which is itself a fragment of the paramatman, the universal self. So, just as we repair and maintain a vehicle for as long as it functions but replace it once it ceases to serve its purpose, the body too was seen as something that eventually wears out with time. And when it perished, the soul was believed to move on to another body and another life, continuing its journey through new earthly experiences.

To develop this understanding, the ancient thinkers often drew inspiration from nature. They observed, for instance, how a serpent sheds its old and worn skin in order to continue living in a renewed one. In the same way, they believed that the soul sheds the body and assumes another form. By recognising the soul as the true identity and the body as merely its outer covering, they sought to overcome the deepest fear of human existence—the fear of death. This profound idea was instilled from childhood, enabling individuals to live with courage, acceptance, and a sense of inner freedom.

The Katha Upanishad tells the allegorical story of a young boy named Nachiketas, who learns about the true nature of death, the self, and the ultimate reality directly from Yama, the god of death.

The story begins when Vajashravas, Nachiketas' father, sought blessings from the gods by giving away his possessions as part of a ritual. Nachiketas noticed that his father was offering only worthless or unproductive items, such as lame, barren, or old cattle. Perplexed, the boy repeatedly asked why his father was doing so.

Seeking the best outcome for his father's rites, Nachiketas finally asked, 'I too am yours. To which god will you offer me?'

Irritated by the persistent questioning, Vajashravas replied in anger, 'I give you unto Yama, the god of death himself.' Though he immediately regretted his words and asked the boy to forget them, Nachiketas treated his father's statement with utmost reverence and resolved to honour it.

Undeterred by his father's resistance, the young boy journeyed to Yama's abode. There, he waited for several days before finally meeting the god of death, from whom he received profound wisdom about death, the self, and the ultimate reality, the Brahman.

Beyond revealing deep cosmic truths, the story of Nachiketas emphasises the importance of cultivating awareness of these profound ideas from childhood. It also demonstrates the remarkable capacity of children to understand and absorb even the deepest philosophical insights.

Antyeshti: The Final Rituals

In ancient India, death was approached with the same care, reverence, and ritual precision as life itself. Funerary practices were designed not only to honour the departed but also to guide the soul safely on its journey beyond the physical world. These beliefs were expressed through a carefully structured sequence of rituals. The funerary rites, known as *antyeshti*, begin with bathing the mortal body in pristine water. The body is then anointed with natural perfume, draped in clean white linen, and laid on a clean white cloth on the ground in the north-south direction. The spiritual reason behind it is that Yama, the god of death, is the guardian of the southern direction, and the body's feet are placed towards the south to facilitate its journey towards Yama's abode. Moreover, the soul is a high energy being and placing the body in the north-south direction, aligned with the earth's magnetic field, is believed to facilitate the prana or life energy to leave the body and merge with the universal energy.

The body is then adorned with fresh, fragrant flowers and sacred Tulsi or basil leaves. Also, a lamp is lit near the person's head with the light facing south. This symbolises the journey of the luminous soul towards the absolute light. After the body is kept for family and friends to come and pay their last respects, a few drops of water from the sacred river Ganga or any of her tributaries are dripped into the deceased person's mouth. The body is then carried to the cremation ground for the final journey of this life.

At the cremation ground, the funeral pyre is first sanctified by sprinkling holy water and chanting mantras for the smooth journey of the soul to the eternal realms. The pyre is then lit, and the family remains there until it has completely burnt out. A small earthen pot filled with ash is then collected from the pyre, after which the family and loved ones return home. A key point to note here is that although cremation was the most prevalent method, the ancient Indians, as in every other aspect of life, were diverse and inclusive in their choices. Hence, burial practices, including inhumation in graves and cave burials, also existed in ancient India.

Beyond the method of laying the body to rest, ancient customs also guided how the living were to respond to the loss. The family members of the deceased remained at home for the next seven days as a period of mourning. This also functioned as a kind of quarantine to ensure the safety of the people in the village or city in case the deceased had suffered from any contagious illness. Since this practice was woven into ritual observance, people strictly adhered to the rule of confinement. During this period, they followed a very simple diet, avoiding spices and heat-inducing ingredients. Rice, often boiled without salt and garnished with milk or lentils, especially *moong dal*, was one of the most common dishes.

Such simple foods have a cooling and soothing effect and help the grieving process.

Notably, the food was symbolically offered to the deceased person as well, signifying that the bond they shared is beyond the body and beyond mortality. It became a way of acknowledging the spiritual unity of souls.

After two weeks, on the thirteenth or sixteenth day, depending on geographical traditions, the entire community was invited for a feast marking the migration of the soul to the eternal worlds. The family then released the ashes into the holy waters of a river or sea. This final act symbolised the merging of the individual's *pancha bhuta* (five great elements) with the cosmic pancha bhuta, signifying a return to and unity with the universe.

Moreover, the ancient Indians often built a small shrine for the deceased and lit a lamp there every morning or evening, much like they did for their deities. This was their way of acknowledging the divinity of the soul once it had left the mortal cage of the body. It also signified reverence for the departed family member, especially an ancestor, and honoured the timeless bond they shared. This simple yet touching routine shows how deeply ancient Indians valued familial bonds and how they made sincere efforts to preserve them even beyond the finality of death.

The Pancha Bhuta: From Elements to Eternity

In ancient India, fire and the natural elements were not merely physical phenomena but sacred forces that guided both daily life and life's final passage. From birth to death, rituals were designed to honour these elements and recognise the interconnectedness of all existence.

This reverence for the elements and their spiritual significance can be seen in one of the most ancient written texts in the world, as well as one of the earliest sources of knowledge, the Rigveda, which begins with an invocation to the fire deity. Fire was regarded as the all-purifying element of nature. Hence, the ancient Indians performed the most important events of life in the presence of fire, treating it as the sacred witness to human actions. During these rituals, they offered clarified butter (ghee), herbs, and other natural substances into the fire as sacred offerings.

An interesting fact here is that in death, the body itself becomes the final offering to the fire deity, the last offering one makes in this life. This is why the ancient Indians predominantly cremated their dead.

Additionally, the ancient Indian largely believed that every being, living or non-living, was composed of the five great elements known as the pancha bhuta: *prithvi* (earth), *jala* (water), *agni* (fire), *vayu* (air), and *akasha* (space or ether). They held that these elements were intimately connected to each being, and that in the end, the individual would return to them. Thus, during the funerary rites, these five elements symbolically come together once again, allowing the body to dissolve back into the very elements from which it arose.

In this way, death was understood not as an end, but as a quiet return to the elemental foundations of existence. Through the five great elements, the body gently returned to the universe from which it had first emerged, completing the natural cycle.

Shraaddham: A Ritual that Connects Galaxies

Shraaddham was a sublime ritual performed by ancient Indians to pay homage to their *pitr*, the departed ancestors. Although birthday celebrations were not widely observed, the death anniversaries of loved ones were honoured with great reverence, for they were regarded as the birth anniversaries of the soul's existence beyond the body. Accordingly, shraaddham was observed each year on the death anniversary of the departed.

Usually performed on the banks of a river or by the seashore, often near a Vishnu temple, the ritual served as a means of remembering the ancestors, offering them symbolic nourishment, and supporting their journey in the higher realms. Offerings of food (*pindam*) and water (*tarpanam*) were made to the departed. The pindam consisted of a ball of cooked rice mixed with black sesame seeds. The rice symbolised purity and nourishment, while sesame seeds represented eternity.

During the ritual, the person performing it—typically a descendant of the deceased—wore a unique ring on the ring finger of the right hand. Known as *pavitram*, meaning sacred, this ring was fashioned from the auspicious and purifying *kusha* or *darbha* grass (*Desmostachya bipinnata*). It was tied in the shape of infinity and worn throughout the ceremony, symbolising the endless cycle of births, deaths, and rebirths through which the soul journeyed across lifetimes. After the offerings of pindam and tarpanam were completed, the performer removed the ring, untied the loop of infinity, and cast the grass into the water. This act symbolised the breaking of the cycle of birth and death and the release of the soul into the eternal realms, where it merged with the One.

Following this, the descendant clapped his wet hands, calling upon the ancestors to accept the offerings. Ancient Indians believed that crows represented the departed souls returning across worlds to receive these offerings. Known for their longevity and their close association with human settlements, crows were thought to witness multiple generations. They lived among people, fed on what was offered, and helped keep the surroundings clean. For these reasons, they were regarded as a symbolic bridge between the living and the departed. When the descendant clapped his wet hands, crows and ravens would arrive, partake of the rice balls, and then fly away.

Apart from individual observances, shraaddham was also performed collectively for the entire community of ancestors during the sacred period in the month of *ashadha*. This honoured not only those who had passed away within living memory but also those who had lived generations earlier—known and unknown, remembered and forgotten. On these days, vast numbers of people gathered along riverbanks and seashores across India to perform the ritual, which also involved the offering of food to countless crows.

The ritual was observed annually because ancient Indians believed that a single day in the realm of the departed equalled

365 days on earth. In this way, they felt they were nourishing their ancestors every day. Thus, shraaddham brought together spirituality, enduring familial affection, and a compassionate act of feeding birds, reflecting both the emotional depth and ecological sensitivity embedded in ancient Indian traditions.

Takeaways from the Ancient Past

- Viewing death not as an end but as a moment in the flow of time when the eternal soul discards an old body and moves on to another life cultivates calmness and helps overcome the fear of death.
- Observing a period of quarantine during the week of mourning reflects both spiritual sensitivity and practical wisdom, helping contain any possible contagion the deceased might have carried.
- Remembering departed ancestors through simple daily prayers and revering them with gratitude nurtures a continuing bond across generations, extending family relationships beyond the mortal realm.

Chapter 17

FREEDOM AND LIBERATION

'You are the solitary witness of all that is, forever free.
Your only bondage is not seeing this.'
—Ashtavakra Gita

Moksha: The Ultimate Freedom

Ancient Indians believed that the entire human life is a journey towards perfection, a divine perfection that always remains just one step away. This elusive nature of ultimate perfection is what keeps human beings striving towards it each day. They called this difficult-to-attain state *moksha*.

Derived from the Sanskrit root word '*muc*,' meaning to 'free,' 'to let go,' 'liberate,' or 'release,' moksha is the state of ultimate freedom from all the fetters of the world. But a question naturally arises here: what are these fetters from which the ancient Indians sought freedom so earnestly? To understand this intricate idea, it is helpful to examine it on two levels: an overarching philosophical level and a more immediate, event-by-event level.

At the philosophical level, the ancient seers referred to the world by the Sanskrit term *samsaara*, meaning the endless cyclicity of existence, or simply, running around in circles. From waking up to sleeping and waking again, from spring through summer, autumn, and winter to the next spring, from birth to death and rebirth, from one life to another, humans appear to move endlessly through these repeating cycles. This does not mean that the ancient Indians failed to appreciate the simple joys and beauty of life. However, they deeply understood the impermanent nature of these experiences and sought something greater, something eternal beyond the transient pleasures and pains of life. They did not wish to remain merely as bodies carried along by time, helplessly moving through these endless cycles. Recognising that no one can truly escape these repeating patterns, it was from this samsaara that they ultimately longed to be free.

At the level of everyday experience, humans are constantly influenced by emotions. We rejoice when we are happy, cry when we are sad, grow agitated when we are angry, and tremble when we are afraid. We move through life never fully knowing what the next moment will bring, and often not even knowing how we ourselves will react to it. Each day becomes a repetition of such uncertainties.

This constant interplay between the unpredictability of events and the unpredictability of our own reactions can make us feel like slaves to our emotions. It is this dimension of samsaara from which the ancient thinkers also sought liberation.

To summarise, the ancient Indians wished to evolve into the highest version of themselves, a state in which sadness and happiness, wealth and poverty, aloneness and togetherness, birth and death could all be perceived with the same calm clarity. They aspired to attain equanimity, a state in which changes in the external world would no longer disturb the internal world. And to reach such a state, one must move beyond the temporary concerns of the material world and understand the true nature of the self.

In the next section, we will explore how ancient Indian thought described the path to attaining complete self-realisation.

The Journey to Self-Realisation: Jnana, Bhakti, and Karma Yoga

In ancient Indian philosophy, the ultimate aim of life was not merely material success but the realisation of a deeper spiritual truth. This quest for self-realisation forms the foundation of the idea of moksha, or liberation.

The Katha Upanishad says, 'He who sees the difference between one being and another goes from death to death.' In other words, as long as we remain deeply attached to 'my life' and 'my possessions,' and view all other beings as separate from ourselves, we remain trapped in the endless cycle of existence. To transcend this, one must realise that the same essence exists in all beings, that the individual self and the ultimate reality are not separate.

When this realisation dawns, one begins to understand that the One resides within everyone. Upon reaching this state of self-realisation, one becomes ready for moksha, ready to free oneself from the endless mechanistic cycle and experience unity with the universe.

However, moksha should not be misunderstood as death. Attaining moksha does not mean that a person abandons the body and floats through the universe as pure energy. Moksha, when experienced while one is still alive, signifies the complete dissolution of the ego. In this state, the sense of a separate self fades away, and the individual begins to experience a profound, selfless love and compassion for all beings.

Therefore, the quest for such self-realisation was supported by clearly articulated spiritual approaches. Ancient Indian philosophy identifies three principal paths, or yogas, through which an individual may attain self-realisation. Each path corresponds to a different temperament and inclination.

1. **Jnana Yoga**

   This is the path of knowledge. Through learning, reflection, and deep inquiry, a seeker gradually acquires wisdom and comes to understand the true nature of reality and the self.

2. **Bhakti Yoga**

   This is the path of devotion. Through wholehearted love and devotion to a chosen deity, the seeker surrenders the ego, allowing the boundary between the self and the divine to dissolve.

3. **Karma Yoga**

   This is the path of action. By performing one's duties without attachment to the results, the seeker rises above personal gain and works for the welfare of all, gradually realising the underlying unity of existence.

Accordingly, those who possessed an intellectual inclination or a deep passion for learning could choose the path of *jnana*. Those who preferred the solace, protection, and comfort of a deity, and who found joy in communicating with a higher power, chose the path of *bhakti*. Ancient texts beautifully express this idea; those who follow *bhakti marga* wish to taste the honey that is God, whereas those who follow *jnana marga* realise that they themselves are that honey. Lastly, those who were naturally inclined towards selfless and dispassionate service chose the *karma marga*.

Thus, for the ancient Indians, the journey towards self-realisation was not a vague or abstract pursuit. Instead, they laid out clearly defined paths suited to different temperaments and personalities. Yet within these paths, there was immense individual freedom. One could walk them in one's own way and at one's own pace. In this sense, they granted individual freedom in the journey towards cosmic freedom.

Another remarkable feature of the Indian belief system is that it did not centre on the idea of an antagonist to God. There was no supreme opposing force whose purpose was to introduce evil into the world. For ancient Indians, the divine encompassed the thesis, the antithesis, and the synthesis. There was no external villain upon whom one could blame one's actions. Each individual was seen as fully responsible for his or her own conduct.

The Bhagavad Gita says, 'You are what you believe in. You become that which you believe you can become.' In this view, life was not a struggle to escape sin or flee from evil. Rather, it was a self-motivated and conscious effort to live righteously. The direction of one's life and destiny lay firmly within one's own actions.

All this highlights how ancient Indian thought placed both freedom and responsibility in the hands of the individual. By recognising one's inner potential and acting with awareness, the journey towards self-realisation becomes not a distant ideal, but a conscious way of living.

Takeaways from the Ancient Past

- Understanding moksha as the ultimate freedom from the endless cycle of samsaara encourages us to look beyond the temporary pleasures and pains of life and seek a deeper, more enduring truth.
- Recognising how emotions and external events constantly influence our reactions highlights the importance of cultivating equanimity, where the inner world remains calm despite changing circumstances.
- Reflecting on the idea that the same essence exists in all beings inspires a shift from ego and separation towards compassion, unity, and a broader sense of connectedness with the universe.
- Exploring the three paths of jnana, bhakti, and karma yoga reminds us that the journey towards self-realisation can take different forms, allowing each individual to pursue spiritual growth according to their temperament and inclination.

EPILOGUE

'Thou art that.'
—Chandogya Upanishad

Now that we have explored the daily life, rituals, practices, and philosophical foundations of an ancient Indian from the beginning of this journey, a remarkable pattern begins to emerge. From the moment they woke up until they entered the realm of sleep, from the first breath taken to the last breath released, their lives were thoughtfully designed to cultivate the profound quality of equanimity. Through aligning themselves with the elements of nature, balancing the body and the mind, pursuing knowledge, practising universal love, and engaging in steadfast action, each day became a quiet step towards inner balance. What may appear at first glance as a collection of rituals and customs was, in reality, a carefully integrated way of life aimed at nurturing harmony within the individual and with the world around them.

Thus, the life of an ancient Indian can be seen as a majestic journey towards one's highest self. It was a path on which one gradually realised that the entire universe exists within oneself, even while continuing to live and act within it, untouched by its turbulence and guided by compassion in one's actions. Such a vision represents a remarkable union of humility in recognising one's place within the vast cosmos and empowerment in understanding that the same cosmic essence resides within the self. Few conceptions of human life are as profound or as inspiring, for they invite each individual to live with awareness, balance, and a deep sense of connection with all existence.

ACKNOWLEDGEMENTS

'Relationships are bound by debts of gratitude.'
—Mahabharata

Krtajnata, or gratitude, has been deeply embedded in the Indian collective consciousness since time immemorial. Therefore, it is only fitting that this book concludes with an expression of thanks to the many people whose support, guidance, and goodwill made it possible.

When aspiring authors often struggle for years to find a publisher willing to accept their work, it felt nothing short of providential that a prestigious publishing house such as Hay House India discovered me through my Instagram channel. I extend my profound gratitude to the wonderful Hay House team, especially Aditya Jarial, for believing in me and in this work and for his thoughtful editing of the manuscript.

This book would not have come to life without the encouragement and appreciation of the hundreds of thousands of followers and the tens of millions of viewers of my Instagram channel. Your curiosity, engagement, and enthusiasm for Indian history and philosophy have continually inspired me to explore deeper and communicate more clearly.

To my dear friends—Aswathy Vinod and Febna Reheem—thank you for the creative brainstorming sessions during the early stages of this book. I am deeply grateful to Igor Zhadnov, Alef Alamayehu, Moshe Blumenthal, Daisy Sebastian, Pranesh Sharma, and Waqas Hyder for the healthy, intense, and often spirited spiritual debates we have shared over the years. Those discussions challenged my assumptions and helped sharpen my understanding of ancient history and philosophy. Thank you, JK (P. Jayakumar), for the unfathomable opportunities you gave me to expand my intellectual horizons. Mohan Subramaniam, thank you for coming into my life at the right time. You are a creative mentor I will cherish all my life. I also extend my heartfelt thanks to Suseela Gauri. You proved that the bonds we forge in life can be as strong as those of blood.

I would also like to thank Dr J. P. Prajith, assistant professor in the department of oriental research and manuscripts library at the University of Kerala, for his insightful interpretations of several rare Sanskrit terms that appear in this work. My special thanks also go to Rahul Jayasree, the remarkable mural artist who brought my vision to life through the cover design.

I wish to acknowledge, with reverence, the countless authors, commentators, and scholars of the extraordinary corpus of Indian literature, from the Vedas to the most contemporary books and research articles. Their work illuminated the path that guided my own exploration. Though we have never met, they remain among the most important teachers in my intellectual journey.

To my brothers—Aarish and Ambareesh—thank you for appreciating and unconditionally embracing all my idiosyncrasies. I cannot imagine a better team to walk through life with.

Finally, I express my deepest gratitude to destiny for allowing me to be born in India, a civilisation whose intellectual, philosophical, and spiritual heritage continues to shape and inspire humanity.

HAY HOUSE

CONNECT WITH
HAY HOUSE
ONLINE

hayhouse.co.in

@hayhouseindia

@hayhouseindia

@hayhouseindia

Join the conversation about latest products, events, exclusive offers, contests, giveaways and more.

'The gateways to wisdom and knowledge are always open.'

Louise Hay